P9-AZV-460

ALSO BY ANN BAUSUM

Stonewall: Breaking Out in the Fight for Gay Rights

the fight against **AIDS** in america

VIRAL

ANN BAUSUM

VIKING

VIKING

An imprint of Penguin Random House LLC, New York

First published in the United States of America by Viking,
an imprint of Penguin Random House LLC, 2019

Copyright © 2019 by Ann Bausum

Penguin supports copyright. Copyright fuels creativity, encourages diverse voices, promotes
free speech, and creates a vibrant culture. Thank you for buying an authorized edition
of this book and for complying with copyright laws by not reproducing, scanning, or
distributing any part of it in any form without permission. You are supporting writers
and allowing Penguin to continue to publish books for every reader.

Visit us online at penguinrandomhouse.com

LIBRARY OF CONGRESS CATALOGING-IN-PUBLICATION DATA
Names: Bausum, Ann, author.
Title: Viral : the fight against AIDS in America / Ann Bausum.
Description: New York : Viking, Penguin Group, [2019] | Audience: 12+ |
Audience: Grade 9 to 12.
Identifiers: LCCN 2018044489 (print) | LCCN 2018047947 (ebook)
ISBN 9780425287224 (ebook) | ISBN 9780425287200 (hardback)
Subjects: LCSH: AIDS (Disease)—United States—Juvenile literature. |
AIDS (Disease)—United States—History—Juvenile literature.
Classification: LCC RA644.A25 (ebook) | LCC RA644.A25 B385 2019 (print) |
DDC 362.19697/9200973—dc23
LC record available at https://lccn.loc.gov/2018044489

Printed in the United States   Set in Berling LT Std   Book design by Kate Renner

1   3   5   7   9   10   8   6   4   2

Cover caption: Participants hold signs at a memorial service in New York's Central Park,
June 13, 1983. Each number represented someone who had died of HIV/AIDS.

R0455907188

For Barbara Cornell,
mother of my friend Michael Riesenberg (1958–1993),
and for all the mothers
and fathers
and grandparents
and sisters
and brothers
and lovers
and spouses
and daughters
and sons
and nieces
and nephews
and uncles
and aunts
and friends
and coworkers
and doctors
and nurses
and caregivers
and strangers
who lost people they knew to AIDS.
And who still do.

CONTENTS

PROLOGUE

"HE has slimming disease," Nigerians told the American medical worker in 1964 when they took her to see a sick man from their village in Africa.

Local residents escorted Judith Williams to an isolated hut on the edge of their community and introduced her to its lone resident, a man reduced by grave illness to barely more than skin-covered bones.

"He was a monkey hunter," villagers told her. "That is who gets slimming disease, monkey hunters."

Williams asked if there was any hope for the man's recovery.

"No, no, they always die," the locals said. "What happens is, when they start to get sick, we bring them out here and then we take care of them until they die."

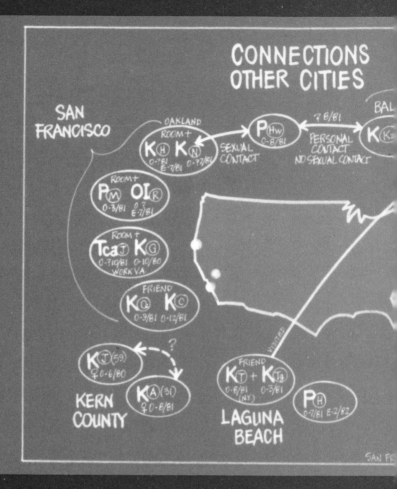

PART ONE
CONTAGION
1969–1983

NEW
YORK

NY.
VACATION

NY
VACATION

SEXUAL
CONTACT
IN N.Y.

LIVED IN
N.Y.

CO

...LIC HEALTH 1982-MARCH

San Francisco Department of
Public Health map showing
the tangled web of mysterious
infections that accompanied
the arrival of what came
to be known as HIV/AIDS,
March 1982.

*"Too much is being transmitted. We've got all
these diseases going unchecked. There are so many
opportunities for transmission that, if something
new gets loose here, we're going to have hell to pay."*

—Dr. Selma Dritz, October 1980

CHAPTER 1

BEFORE

1969–1979

BEFORE 1969 lesbians, gay men, bisexuals, and the cross-dressing pioneers of the transgender movement lived in a world that sought to delegitimize their very existence. Even the term used to categorize them—homosexual—doubled as an epithet. Every religious faith condemned same-sex attraction as sinful. The medical establishment categorized it as a form of mental illness. And authorities criminalized the most intimate of private sexual acts almost uniformly across the United States, even within one's own home. Just dancing with someone of the same sex could lead to arrest. In most places, the only night when an individual could safely assume a persona from the opposite gender was on Halloween.

Such conditions pushed people deep into metaphorical closets and toward tragic self-destructive acts. Oppress people long enough, though, and they may refuse to stay confined. In 1969 those shuttered closet doors burst open during a police raid on a hot June night at the Stonewall Inn, a gay bar in New York City. The raid ignited days of street protests that helped to draw gay people out of isolation and push them toward an affirming sense of community. The

Stonewall riots signaled a collective rejection of past condemnations, and they fueled an embrace of the possibilities of gay liberation in the quest for freedom.

Freedom from oppression.

Freedom to embrace one's identity.

And freedom to embrace one another.

The various strands of what would become the LGBTQ community explored these freedoms in unique ways. Lesbians found strength in a sisterhood of solidarity, whether as couples or as part of the women's liberation fight against the culture's male-dominated power structure. The era's butch lesbians and male transvestites defied the biologically aligned cisgender norms of identity and paved the way for the transgender movement that would follow. Many gay men joined their lesbian, bisexual, and trans allies in an ongoing fight for increased civil and legal rights. A good number of them also pursued trails of personal liberation that often came down to one thing: sex.

Uninhibited, unrestrained sex.

"All of those loves that dare not speak their names, all of those forbidden sex acts," recalled Rodger McFarlane, "were free for the taking" in places like New York City, as he discovered after moving there from rural Alabama. Baby boomers, that abundant population that came of age during the 1960s and 1970s, looked around and found plenty of people ready to explore territory previously shrouded by taboo. For gay men, what they experienced was not just pleasurable, noted McFarlane, it "was also very liberating because it removed shame. It removed shame by the bucketfuls. It replaced shame, in fact, with great joy and self-discovery of your body and other people's, and loving each other and, I mean, all the good stuff about free love."

Free love. The idea that it was okay to enjoy sex with or without emotional bonding, and that someone could love multiple partners simultaneously. Free love. It was heady. It was liberating. And it was fun.

It was also big business.

An urban infrastructure blossomed after Stonewall that supported—and made money from—men having sex with men. During previous decades gay communities had taken root in coastal cities such as New York, San Francisco, and Los Angeles at neighborhood networks of underground gay clubs and bars. During the late 1960s and 1970s, as laws became less restrictive, these businesses came out of hiding, and they multiplied, diversified, and thrived.

There were bars that catered to particular fetishes and attires; clubs where dancing prevailed; places with darkened backrooms; and always, everywhere, the temptation to hook up for sex. Gay men cruised weight-lifting gyms. They visited informal meet-up spots such as the abandoned piers and warehouses of lower Manhattan in New York City. Even during an era where gay people generally remained closeted around coworkers and family, the networks existed for finding like-minded friendship and more.

One of the most enticing places to mingle was in gay bathhouses. Although these establishments had a veneer of respectability about them—offering swimming pools, exercise equipment, steam rooms, showers, a staff of masseurs, live entertainment, and other amenities—the underlying purpose of a bathhouse was unmistakable. "Come to Man's Country," a New York destination advertised, "and develop your body, or a friendship with somebody else's. Visit us once, and you'll come again and again." Someone looking for sex could lounge in a private changing room, door ajar, and wait for a stranger to walk in. "It was simple," recalled writer Larry Kramer. "It was like going into a candy store."

As the 1970s built toward their hedonistic crescendo, disco music took hold and its irresistible, unrelenting beat pulled bodies

Crowds fill the dance floor at Studio 54, November 6, 1979.

into such legendary dance clubs as Studio 54 in the center of New York City or the gay-oriented Saint in lower Manhattan. Illegal drug use was on the rise everywhere, from the straight world to the gay party scene, where it became an essential part of the entertainment. Marijuana, cocaine, LSD, quaaludes, speed, Special K (ketamine), and mescaline were in abundance. So was inhaled amyl nitrite, a tactile-enhancing substance that went by the street name of poppers because of the sound made by breaking open its packaging. More drugs led almost inevitably to more sex. And more sex led to more experimentation.

But even in places like New York City and San Francisco, public displays of same-sex affection drew everything from sidelong glances to violent attacks beyond all but the most tolerant settings. People of color who were gay faced double doses of discrimination and risk. Laws overwhelmingly sided with employers who fired gay

New York City activists march in the first gay pride parade and commemorate the previous year's Stonewall riots, June 28, 1970. Participants included Vito Russo (holding banner, wearing striped pants).

employees, landlords who evicted gay tenants, and businesses that excluded gay customers—all of which happened with disheartening regularity.

In consequence, long before the emergence of the term *safe space*, gay-dominated retreats sprang up at select locations for those who could afford them, including Fire Island, a thirty-mile-long barrier island off the coast of Long Island beyond New York City. The subterranean revelry of nearby Manhattan burst into full bloom under the sunshine and through the endless nights of the island's summer weekends. Private house parties. Beach romances. Group orgies. The possibilities were limited only by the weather and the ferry schedule.

Fire Island wasn't the only such point of refuge. Unfettered by family responsibilities, gay men of means made the rounds to other hot spots on what they called the national gay circuit. Key West, Fort Lauderdale, and Miami's South Beach in Florida. Providence in Rhode Island. California's Castro district in San Francisco, West Hollywood near Los Angeles, and the state's southern desert getaway of Palm Springs. Each hub developed reputations for its own distinctive features, attractions, and not-to-be-missed seasonal parties.

Whether catching the circuit tour, marching in a gay pride parade, or visiting the darkened backrooms of bars, gay men could experience a shared sense of camaraderie, of belonging, and of affirmation that their desires were perfectly okay. Recalling the dance scene on Fire Island, Kramer told documentary filmmaker Joseph Lovett, "It was hard not to feel great love, and trust, and brotherhood, and 'Look at us,' and 'Look, we've made it.'" The rest of society would just have to catch up with the times.

For those most deeply embedded in such environments, unfettered same-sex intercourse became the ultimate statement of liberation. One way to reject past oppression was to ignore all previous boundaries on sexual behavior. For some, the physical act of sexual intercourse broke free from any mooring to deeper emotional attachment. If having some sex equaled liberation, then having more sex surely demonstrated still greater freedom. Even couples in long-term relationships reevaluated mutual commitments of monogamy.

Norms of behavior changed so thoroughly—in terms of intercourse frequency, having sex with strangers, the range of imaginable sex acts, and the use of inhibition-lowering drugs—that, by the end of the '70s, the most sexually active had engaged in multiple forms of intercourse with dozens, or hundreds, or in some cases even thousands of partners.

Such actions were not without consequence.

Sexually transmitted infections raced through local communities and jumped via the gay circuit from point to point and coast to coast. A surge in oral-anal intercourse merely compounded the problem, transforming parasitic intestinal tract illnesses previously associated with poor sanitation into sexually acquired diseases. At the epicenters of infection, people traded illnesses as often as they swapped phone numbers.

Gonorrhea.

Herpes.

Hepatitis.

Syphilis.

Amebiasis.

Giardiasis.

A veritable carousel of disease.

So much disease that it was "too much," as Selma Dritz would tell her medical colleagues in San Francisco in 1980.

Condoms played almost no role in containing any of this transmission because at that time most people saw condoms as having only one function, preventing pregnancy. Anyone who became ill simply turned to healthcare professionals for what was then an expanding arsenal of powerful antibiotics. These drugs seemed capable of curing everything, and they became an almost essential vitamin for the most active participants in the gay male sexual revolution.

"We didn't know we were dancing on the edge of our graves," New York transplant Rodger McFarlane later observed. "It was the headiest experience I've ever had in my life. And it is unrivaled still." Life before Stonewall had been filled with oppression, and life after Stonewall, for many gay men, overflowed with liberation. But that was before what came next.

And what came next was AIDS.

CHAPTER 2

OUTBREAK

1980–1981

THE first to die left behind little more than their names and brief stories of chaotic, terrifying deaths. Individual by individual, they went from being seemingly well to perplexingly ill in a matter of months. Stripped of energy, they succumbed to strange infections, and their youthful physiques melted away until they looked like aged skeletons covered in sagging skin.

No one could believe the men were dying.

Not the sick.

Not their friends.

Not their doctors.

By some counts, Rick Wellikoff was the fourth person in the United States to die because of AIDS, but no one understood in 1980 that that's what had killed him. During the fall of 1979 this grade-school teacher in Brooklyn, New York, sought medical advice about the hardened lymph nodes and odd purple skin rash he'd developed. After some testing, doctors diagnosed his rash as Kaposi's sarcoma, but that was odd because this type of cancer, otherwise known as KS, usually occurred in aging men of Mediterranean ancestry, not someone in his thirties like Wellikoff. As cancers went, doctors viewed KS as relatively harmless; it progressed so slowly that few people actually died of it.

But not this time. Wellikoff's KS spread with surprising speed. Continually exhausted, he quit his job, yet still he got sicker. Before the end of the next year, he didn't just have KS. He'd developed an unusual lung infection, too. The illnesses overran his body, and he died on Christmas Eve 1980, at the age of thirty-seven. A few months later grieving friends scattered his ashes into the Atlantic Ocean as its waves rolled onto the sands of his beloved Fire Island.

The month after Wellikoff's death, a friend and former Fire Island housemate of his died, too. Nick Rock had worked on cruise ships and been a bartender before he'd become worn down and lethargic. He likewise had developed KS. He experienced persistent diarrhea and couldn't maintain his weight. After he suffered a seizure in the fall of 1980, his lover literally carried his diminished partner to a New York City hospital in search of help.

But no matter what physicians tried, instead of getting better, Rock got worse. Doctors said that he had multiple kinds of infections raging throughout his body. In his lungs. In his brain. In his organs. The names were a scientific blur. Toxoplasmosis. Cytomegalovirus, otherwise known as CMV. And some unidentified infection in his lungs. By the end of his short life, white foam was emanating from his mouth, his ears, and his nose. After a series of heart attacks, he died on January 15, 1981.

George Kenneth Horne Jr. hadn't known Rock or Wellikoff. He'd grown up in Oregon and in the mid-1960s had moved to San Francisco at age twenty-one to study ballet. Eventually he'd set aside his ambitions of becoming a professional dancer and taken an office job. He'd also discovered the city's vibrant gay social scene. By the fall of 1980, he'd become ill with the first reported case in San Francisco of what would eventually be called HIV/AIDS.

As the months wore on, his lethargy and skin rash were compounded by constant fevers and debilitating headaches. Doctors had names for his afflictions—KS, CMV, and cryptococcal meningitis—but the usual treatments didn't work. Despite all manner of medical interventions, he just got worse. A few other people began turning up similarly ill and faced equally rapid and frightening deaths. They left behind grieving partners, mystified doctors, and family members who were often astonished to discover a secret the men had not been prepared to reveal: that they were gay.

They were gay.

That was part of what was so perplexing about the earliest cases. Everyone who came down with the inexplicable pattern of illness was gay. "Unusual" was how medical professionals characterized the peculiar coincidence of five previously healthy gay men in Los Angeles coming down with a rare form of pneumonia known as PCP. This assessment accompanied their observations in a brief article published on June 5, 1981, in the newsletter of the US Centers for Disease Control, a publication known as the *MMWR*.

Unusual.

The next month a group of doctors in New York and California described the cases of twenty-six gay men who'd coincidentally developed KS, including the former ballet student Ken Horne. Many had since died. Some were likewise afflicted with PCP. This alert triggered reports from other physicians who had encountered similarly perplexing presentations of illness. Seventy of them. All gay. Many progressing with seeming inevitability toward death. Horne, by the final weeks of his life, had been reduced to 122 pounds, lost the sight in one eye, and begun exhibiting signs of dementia. He died on November 30, 1981.

▲

Not everyone who became ill died immediately. Some people stabilized and returned home, but those who got better did not get well. There was still something wrong with them that doctors didn't understand or know how to treat. It would take decades to make sense of it all. Meanwhile the long-termers survived, seemingly, thanks to healthful living, optimism, and sheer will. "The sure sign of someone who's going to kick the bucket early is someone who turns inward, keeps the fear to themselves," observed Dan Turner, who became ill in San Francisco in early 1982. He would live for another eight years.

But Turner and the other long-termers were the exception. In most cases, despite great medical heroics and expense, healthcare professionals were unable to save their patients' lives—or even understand why they had died. That wasn't supposed to happen in the closing decades of the twentieth century. Doctors had figured out how to transplant organs, end polio, and cure just about everything except cancer. But not this. This situation made no sense.

Analysts from the Centers for Disease Control, known as the CDC, took the lead in trying to find out what could be going on. Recently the center's staffers had solved two high-profile medical mysteries—the 1976 outbreak at a convention in Philadelphia of what became known as Legionnaires' disease and the toxic shock scare of 1980 among menstruating women. The mysteries had been solved by CDC epidemiologists, scientists who specialize in the study and tracking of epidemics. In both cases researchers discovered that already known and treatable bacteria were spreading through unanticipated mechanisms. They identified an air-conditioning system as the culprit in the first occurrence and a new ultra-absorbent brand of tampons in the second. The solutions were simple. Clean the air filtration system. Discontinue using the tampons. Take antibiotics to cure the infections.

The relatively easy containment of these outbreaks, accompanied by ongoing advances in modern medicine, had created a growing sense of confidence, in the medical profession and beyond, that people could control communicable diseases by employing three trusted lines of defense. The practice of good hygiene. The vigilant use of immunity-producing vaccines. And an arsenal of increasingly potent antibiotics.

It seemed as easy as one, two, three.

But, in 1981, epidemiologists quickly realized they were facing a tougher problem. An unusual problem. Even when they began to piece together the patterns of the outbreak—that it affected gay men, that it appeared to be transmitted through sexual intercourse, that it looked as if it remained dormant for some time before striking—they couldn't identify the cause of the malaise. It was as if some new infectious agent was afoot. And it was like nothing they'd ever encountered before.

Later on epidemiologists would realize that a similar pattern of infection was taking hold beyond the gay community. But those cases were too rare or too hidden within marginalized groups for medical professionals to immediately recognize the connections. In consequence, when physicians followed the medical custom of naming the new illness based on its point of origin, they linked it to one community: gay men. GRID: gay-related immune deficiency, many called it. Or sometimes gay compromise syndrome. Others began referring to it informally as gay cancer. Or, even more casually, as Saint's disease, after New York's Saint disco, where so many of the afflicted had once danced.

Even before it became known as GRID, reports of the new illness began to spread. "Rare Cancer Seen in 41 Homosexuals," announced a *New York Times* story that ran during the Fourth of July holiday in 1981. The article particularly caught the attention of gay men, including those visiting Fire Island. For many, it was the first marker in what would become an era dominated by a growing health crisis. According to journalist and AIDS historian David France, vacationers "spent the long weekend examining one another's flesh," in search of the bruise-like blemishes it described.

They found them by the dozens.

That same summer, across the country in San Francisco, a registered nurse named Bobbi Campbell became the city's sixteenth case of KS. Soon after, he began raising an alarm among fellow citizens as a sort of modern-day Paul Revere. But this time it was the gay community that was under attack, and Campbell didn't need a horse. All he needed was a Polaroid camera, writing implements, and some paper.

KS Poster Boy, he called himself.

Campbell started taking Polaroid photographs of his KS lesions and including them in homemade posters that he displayed in the Castro district, the city's gay population hub. He also began writing about his illness and his outreach in the *San Francisco Sentinel*, the local gay newspaper. He called his column the Gay Cancer Journal. Campbell used it to share his own experiences and to report whatever he could learn about the outbreak of the strange cancerous rash.

"I'm writing because I have a determination to live," Campbell affirmed to the paper's readers. "You do too—don't you?" Sometimes he wore a T-shirt calling attention to himself as the Poster Boy so that people would know they could turn to him with questions. He couldn't always offer answers, but he could warn gay men to take charge of their physical health. The marks might look like bruises, but they weren't, Campbell explained. They don't fade away; they spread. They were an ominous sign of major medical trouble, he cautioned, and people should take them seriously. Dead seriously.

Because if you had them you might be about to get deadly sick.

CHAPTER 3

REACTIONS

1981–1982

"I don't think anybody is going to give a damn," a dermatologist told Larry Kramer during the summer of 1981. Alvin Friedman-Kien was one of the New York doctors who had diagnosed the earliest cases of KS in the city. Despite sounding an alarm, however, he and his colleagues hadn't received the customary attention or funding that such an alert would normally merit. The truth was, he suggested, during an era where gays remained largely closeted and marginalized, no one was likely to advocate for gay men who were dying from a cancerous rash and other infections. "It's really up to you guys to do something," he said.

Friedman-Kien implored Kramer to help find funding so that he and others could conduct medical research about the outbreak in the hopes of containing its spread. Kramer, a successful author and playwright, had plenty of connections, but he also had a knack for irritating people with his outspoken manner and opinions. In 1978 he'd infuriated many of his readers with the publication of *Faggots*, a novel that went on to become a classic in the gay community, but that was still provoking outrage three years after its release because of its portrayal of gay men as overly focused on sex. Nonetheless Kramer managed to fill his living room with influential and curious guests on August 11 when he hosted Friedman-Kien for an information and fund-raising session about the outbreak.

Friedman-Kien's appeal for funding met with considerable success. Those in attendance pledged $6,635 on the spot in support of his work with another concerned physician, Joseph Sonnabend. But Friedman-Kien provoked an uproar when he suggested that gay men consider curtailing their sexual intercourse until scientists learned more about what was making them sick. Promiscuity had become the equivalent of liberation for so many gay men that the thought of giving it up was as inconceivable as the idea of returning to the furtive life and shame that had accompanied gay bar raids.

▲

San Francisco public health official Selma Dritz outlines connections relating to the GRID outbreak, circa 1982.

Most gay men, in addition to insisting on their rights to sexual freedom, agreed on another point, too—that the nation needed to include them its promise of equality. They were infuriated by the harassment and discrimination that persisted through the years following the Stonewall riots of 1969. Additional groups expressed similar frustrations, including lesbians, feminists, people of color, and those fighting for trans rights. But these growing campaigns for equality generated alarm among people who clung to older boundaries of class, race, and gender, and a conservative political backlash sprang from their anxieties.

In 1980, Ronald Reagan, a Hollywood actor turned politician and Democrat turned Republican, had become the standard-bearer for this conservative movement during that year's presidential campaign. He and his Republican supporters championed the virtues of the established nuclear family, the values of religious faith, and the importance of spending more money on the nation's Cold War–era military defenses, even if that meant spending less on domestic programs. That November they prevailed at the polls.

In January 1981, just a few months before physicians began filing reports about strange opportunistic infections in gay men, Reagan became the nation's fortieth president. His early acts included cuts to federal spending on medical research and the appointment of conservative directors to government agencies, actions that lay at the root of Friedman-Kien's funding shortfall. As the doctor had told Kramer, nobody in Washington gave a damn if gay men were becoming ill and dying. Some even welcomed this development as proof of their unscientific characterization of homosexuality as a sinful lifestyle choice instead of as the biologically driven orientation it's been proven to be.

"The poor homosexuals—they have declared war upon nature, and now nature is exacting an awful retribution," conservative commentator Pat Buchanan would go on to write. As the crisis worsened, hate crimes increased against members of the gay community. Some of the most outspoken critics went so far as to suggest that branding, quarantine, and even capital punishment were the appropriate responses to the outbreak, not medical intervention.

Nobody gave a damn.

Clusters of officials at the CDC tried repeatedly to break through the overwhelming silence, condemnation, or indifference that accompanied the mysterious infections. Others raised alarms, too, including New York physician Lawrence Mass, who had begun authoring local alerts from the very beginning of the outbreak in an effort to educate fellow gays about the seriousness of the threat. Larry Kramer became increasingly exasperated when cases of GRID continued to mount without any reaction from the Reagan administration. In January 1982 he turned his apartment into a meeting space once again. This time what emerged was Gay Men's Health Crisis, otherwise known as GMHC.

This new organization sought to close the care gap that was developing in the absence of federal action. More and more gay men were becoming ill and dying, and they were doing so without the necessary infrastructure to meet their needs. GMHC became that support system. It matched volunteers with tasks as simple as caring for pets while someone was in the hospital and as grave as helping to draft wills for those preparing to die. Lawyers and artists, gay men and lesbians, straight women and men, the wealthy and those of modest means all stepped up to help.

One of the group's earliest volunteers was Rodger McFarlane. McFarlane proved to be a particularly dedicated and capable helper. On his own initiative, he set up the first ever hotline for the syndrome using an answering machine connected to his home phone. Soon this former technician for a US Navy nuclear submarine became GMHC's first paid director. He deftly organized the group's growing cadre of helpers into a buddy system of support. Lawyers advocated for tenants whose landlords had evicted them because of their illnesses. Other volunteers helped the homebound with shopping, cleaning, and cooking. When conditions worsened, they held hands with the sick and offered palliative care to the dying.

The organization posted what it called a rest-in-peace list of deceased clients whenever someone died. Before long, such accountings were emerging daily. "Sometimes the list is more than a dozen names, filling a whole sheet," GMHC lawyer Mark Senak told a friend. "We were forced to take care of ourselves," McFarlane explained the year after GMHC's founding, "because we learned that if you have certain diseases, certain lifestyles, you can't expect the same services as other parts of society."

Similar efforts took hold in epicenters of the crisis on the West Coast. In San Francisco, for example, the already-established Shanti Project helped to meet the needs of the dying through its subsidized housing program and peer volunteer services. Such efforts on the two coasts were "the first case, I think, in history where the actual afflicted people are taking control, taking charge of the epidemic," Larry Kramer later observed.

Poster Boy Bobbi Campbell extended his advocacy work in San Francisco with the help of his drag activist group, the Sisters of Perpetual Indulgence. Starting in 1979 members had periodically donned nun habits for street performances and other outreach that was designed to dispel LGBTQ stigmas. In 1982 Campbell, otherwise known as Sister Florence Nightmare, collaborated with other members, including fellow activist and registered nurse Baruch Golden, aka Sister Roz Erection, to create a peer-written guide to safer sex. They called it *Play Fair!* Employing snappy humor and sex-positive language, the cartoon-illustrated pamphlet encouraged men to use condoms as a way to limit the spread of sexually transmitted infections. Their publication included a warning about the recent emergence of the opportunistic infections associated with GRID.

In the pre-Internet days of the 1980s, gay people on the East and West Coasts worked more independently and focused on their local communities. Even so their efforts followed parallel paths, whether in community care or advocacy, because GRID created similar challenges. Starting in November 1982, gay friends Michael Callen and Richard Berkowitz launched an information campaign in New York City that was reminiscent of Bobbi Campbell's early work in San Francisco. Both Callen and Berkowitz exhibited symptoms associated with the outbreak and were concerned because so many gay New Yorkers were dismissing their risks of infection and the consequences of becoming ill.

"We know who we are," the twenty-seven-year-olds wrote, "and we know why we're sick." They prefaced their pronouncement in the *New York Native* gay newspaper by calling out, "Those of us who have lived a life of excessive promiscuity on the urban gay circuit of bathhouses, backrooms, balconies, sex clubs, meat racks, and tearooms." Such behavior needed to stop, they said. Callen and Berkowitz realized their recommendations weren't for everyone: "For some, perhaps homosexuality will always mean promiscuity. They may very well die for that belief." The coauthors introduced that statement by observing: "The motto of promiscuous gay men has been 'So many men, so little time.' In the '70s we were worried about so many men; in the '80s we will have to worry about so little time. For us, the party that was the '70s is over."

Some months earlier, Congressman Henry Waxman of California had held a regional hearing in Los Angeles to learn more about the health concerns in his home district. His was the first congressional inquiry into GRID. During the session James Curran, the physician coordinating the CDC's epidemiological research, warned Waxman that the outbreak seen so far was "merely the tip of the iceberg, that there may be tens of thousands of men who have milder breakdowns or milder compromises in their immune systems."

Bobbi Campbell (kneeling, center) cavorts with other members of the Sisters of Perpetual Indulgence, circa 1983.

Despite this ominous alert and reports from other experts on how spending cuts were hampering research at the CDC and elsewhere, neither the Reagan administration nor members of Congress authorized additional spending to address GRID. Nor did the alarms prompt federal legislators to convene further hearings about the matter.

▲

By the 1980s new technologies had made it possible for physicians to evaluate the health of a person's immune system by measuring a recently discovered component named the T cell. Healthy T cell readings were 600 or better, but tests on people with GRID came far below normal. These results helped to confirm that someone's symptoms fit the pattern of the illness, but it couldn't explain why people with low counts developed opportunistic infections or why existing treatments for those infections failed to work.

There was no shortage of theories. Maybe there'd been a bad batch of poppers, and gay men had become ill from using the illegal inhalant. Maybe a microorganism was lurking in the plumbing of the bathhouses. Maybe gay men had worn out their immune systems. Maybe they had developed resistance to antibiotics by overusing them. Maybe excessive promiscuity itself had somehow triggered the outbreak.

During the summer of 1982 researchers had been forced to abandon these lines of inquiry after the CDC learned of thirty-four cases that matched all the characteristics of GRID except for one. These individuals insisted they were not gay. Most were hemophiliacs. Some admitted using the injectable street drug heroin. A few had received blood transfusions during surgeries. One of the cases was female. All of this evidence prompted the CDC to update its name for the outbreak. That September the designation of GRID—gay-related immune deficiency—was reclassified as acquired immune deficiency syndrome, and, later, acquired immunodeficiency syndrome. Either way the acronym was the same.

AIDS.

The name change didn't reflect any greater understanding of what was causing the illness, but, in the months that followed, epidemiologists became increasingly convinced that an unidentified virus was spreading the infection via contaminated human blood. Injecting drug users routinely economized by sharing needles, a sure way to pass around blood-borne infections. Sexual intercourse often resulted in imperceptible abrasions that exposed partners to each other's blood. Surgical patients depended on blood transfusions, and hemophiliacs relied on products derived from whole blood. Such blood supplies went through a filtering process to reduce the risk of passing infectious bacteria from donors to recipients, but researchers knew viruses were so small that they slipped through.

Further evidence of the transmission link between AIDS and blood came to light in December 1982. That month Selma Dritz was among the health professionals in San Francisco who tracked the case of an infant with AIDS to a blood transfusion the child had received from a previously healthy donor. That donor also had subsequently developed the syndrome. This connection represented what Dritz called "the nail in the coffin" on the ability of whatever was causing AIDS to travel through the blood. How else could the infection have reached this child? And if this child had contracted AIDS from a blood transfusion, who else might be doing the same?

Some months earlier James Curran had warned that investigators were seeing only the tip of the iceberg when it came to infections. By year's end, it was clear that AIDS was no ordinary iceberg. Its potential to spread was assuming the proportions of a monstrosity.

But beyond the front lines, nobody gave a damn.

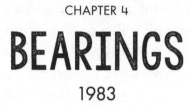

CHAPTER 4

BEARINGS

1983

IN March 1983, under a screaming headline, "1,112 and Counting," Larry Kramer implored readers of the *New York Native* to start paying attention to the escalating spread of illness. "If this article doesn't scare the shit out of you, we're in real trouble," he began. "If this article doesn't rouse you to anger, fury, rage, and action, gay men may have no future on this earth. Our continued existence depends on just how angry you can get." Kramer informed the *Native*'s gay readership that the outbreak was expanding exponentially and had infected more than a thousand people nationwide. New Yorkers accounted for almost half of these cases, and nearly two hundred of the five hundred-some known deaths, he noted.

Kramer had known twenty of the deceased New York men, and he listed their names in tribute, starting with Nick Rock and Rick Wellikoff. "If we don't act immediately, then we face our approaching doom," he warned. His comments failed to stir mass action, but a few others were beginning to have similar concerns. When author Toby Marotta shared a 1983 *New York Times* editorial about the outbreak with a gay friend, he confided, "I think it's the toughest issue we've yet faced."

By March it had become patently obvious to CDC epidemiologists and others at the heart of the crisis that the vector behind the AIDS outbreak traveled via blood. The recently uncovered connection between a blood-transfused infant and blood donor in San Francisco provided ironclad proof. No one knew how long the infectious agent could hide inside a person before symptoms of illness emerged. It was possible that seemingly healthy blood donors were unwittingly passing the pathogen to blood recipients who were equally unaware of their proximity to it.

The nation's entire blood delivery system was at risk.

Since the 1940s Americans have depended upon stockpiles of human blood during injury, surgery, and the treatment of illness. CDC staffers had begun making the case in July 1982 that donors could be inadvertently contaminating these supplies, and their concerns increased whenever additional groups of people began to exhibit the same patterns of illness as the ones affecting gay men. Some people used the catchy but offensive phrase "Four-H Club" to label this expanding circle of infection: in addition to homosexual men, AIDS had emerged among heroin users, hemophiliacs, and, in an outbreak that would remain inexplicable for decades, recent Haitian immigrants. Soon the web expanded to include women who had had sexual intercourse with infected intravenous drug users as well as children born to these women.

Then, as now, a decentralized network of independent organizations and firms shared responsibility for the nation's blood supplies, not the federal government. Despite mounting evidence in 1982 that the country's reserves were at risk, no one in the Reagan administration issued any rule changes that would have helped to protect them, and Congress passed no new laws and opened no investigations into the matter. Meanwhile, those entities responsible for collection and management of blood components resisted calls to adjust their policies voluntarily, including the American Red Cross, other blood banks, and the pharmaceutical firms that bundled and sold blood products such as the clotting factor used by hemophiliacs.

These groups worried that it might be hard to maintain the ideal inventory of blood if they began to turn away previously reliable donors, including members of the gay community, and they predicted they could face charges of discrimination if they refused donations from certain segments of the population. Why not wait and act on fuller knowledge, they suggested. Surely researchers would identify the cause of the infection soon. That way collectors could avoid the hassle and expense of retooling their methods until they knew exactly what pathogen to target during screening.

After nine months of frustrating circular arguments with these private partners, the CDC turned directly to the public for help in securing the nation's blood supply. Starting in March of 1983 patients with scheduled surgeries were encouraged to make advance donations of their own blood in case they needed transfusions during their medical procedures. In addition, the CDC requested that members of populations at high risk of infection voluntarily discontinue donating their blood.

Going forward, the CDC asked all donors to sign a form asserting that they did not belong to one of those six high-risk groups: the symptomatic; homosexual and bisexual men with multiple sexual partners (which counted as two groups); recent Haitian immigrants; individuals with a history of intravenous drug use; and sexual partners of any of these risk groups. A statement that accompanied the 1983 form admitted that scientists understood almost nothing about AIDS, only that "it is known to be fatal and that currently specific treatment is unknown."

Two months later Congress finally allocated some dedicated funding for AIDS research. By then a syndrome that had started

Marchers carry a banner in New York City's gay pride parade, June 26, 1983. Organizers dedicated that year's march to the memory of the 644 people who had died of AIDS, almost half of whom had lived in New York City.

with a few localized outbreaks had assumed the markers of an epidemic, having spread to thirty-four states and fifteen foreign countries. "Don't say there wasn't enough money," New York oncologist Linda Laubenstein corrected a reporter the month after the modest appropriation of $12 million. When describing the nation's initial response to AIDS, she said, "Say there wasn't any money."

Funding hadn't been the only deterrent to research during the first two years of the crisis. Few scientists had felt drawn to study what had begun as a relatively small outbreak within a stigmatized population, and those who did take up the challenge had little idea of what they were looking for or where to find it. Research began in earnest only after the CDC had identified an unknown blood-borne virus as the likely cause for AIDS some eighteen months into the crisis. As this effort gained momentum, much of it occurred at the government's National Institutes of Health, but scientists worked elsewhere, too, including at the CDC and at university labs such as the medical school of the University of California in San Francisco.

Because AIDS was emerging in other regions of the world, international researchers also joined the effort, including those at the Pasteur Institute in Paris. This French team, headed by virologist Luc Montagnier, made the first scientific breakthrough when it uncovered a previously unknown virus in the tissues of people with AIDS. This discovery demonstrated the crucial contributions that scientists from the new field of microbiology could make, aided by such cutting-edge technologies as scanning electron microscopes and machines capable of sorting and counting specific types of cells. The finding also created a new avenue for research: determining whether the presence of the new pathogen was a mere coincidence or a possible cause for the syndrome.

▲

In 1981, during the opening months of the outbreak, doctors had begun conferring with colleagues around the country on possible treatment strategies. By 1983 their patients and allies were doing the same, and they discovered how frequently their experiences and responses had aligned. In the same way that the positive-thinking Dan Turner was living longer than expected in San Francisco, Michael Callen was extending his lifespan in New York through, among other things, a determination to remain hopeful. "I don't say hope will guarantee you'll beat AIDS," he asserted, "but you've got to have it to be in the running."

Likewise, in the same way that San Francisco's Sisters of Perpetual Indulgence had sought to raise awareness in 1982 with its *Play Fair!* pamphlet, Callen and his friend Richard Berkowitz had authored a forty-page booklet they called *How to Have Sex in an*

Epidemic: One Approach. Their publication, written before they'd heard of the Sisters' pamphlet, employed a more text-heavy and matter-of-fact tone, but its intent was identical: help people protect themselves from infection. Their physician and friend Joseph Sonnabend added a foreword to the document and served as medical adviser to the work. Callen's lover Richard Dworkin helped review and type drafts.

In painstaking detail and using sex-positive language, authors Callen and Berkowitz outlined the relative risks of every potential sexual act and the precautions that might mitigate or eliminate those risks. No act or topic was taboo. Although some of the scientific theories included in the book failed to prove true—such as the idea that AIDS was the byproduct of an overtaxed immune system instead of a specific infectious agent—the book's practical suggestions were literally life saving.

In the months and years that followed, the two men and others, including GMHC, reprinted, revised, and further reprinted the publication many thousands of times. Eventually *How to Have Sex in an Epidemic* reached a nationwide audience. Some gay men continued to resist its calls for moderation and its relentless advocacy of the use of condoms, but plenty of others welcomed the candor of its advice and followed it.

A month after their booklet's initial printing, Callen and Berkowitz met some of their previously unknown counterparts when they gathered with other gay activists and health professionals at a conference in Denver, Colorado. The forum, which was one of the first national meetings about AIDS, had been organized through the leadership of LGBTQ activist Virginia Apuzzo at what was then called the National Gay Task Force.

Eleven conference attendees exhibited symptoms associated with AIDS, including Callen and Berkowitz from New York, and Dan Turner and Bobbi Campbell from San Francisco. All eleven

were white gay men. The group commiserated and brainstormed amidst the conference's various proceedings and decided on the spot to organize a national association. Their founding statement for People with AIDS became known as the Denver Principles, and its eleven tenets formed the basis for virtually all of the activism and care that followed.

Before the health forum ended, the authors of the Denver Principles seized the stage of the meeting with a banner that read *Fighting for Our Lives* and shared the text of their document. They began with a preamble that introduced the men using their nomenclature of choice: People with AIDS, a phrase soon shortened to "PWA." As PWAs they rejected being labeled "victims" and "patients," they said, because these words suggested passivity and defeat. The points that followed made it clear that they were neither.

Their statement called for fairness in employment and housing, access to healthcare without discrimination, and the development of appropriate social services. It asked others to see PWAs as human

The founders of People with AIDS stand united during their debut in Denver, June 1983. Bobbi Campbell brought their trademark banner from San Francisco where he had helped to make it for a local AIDS memorial march.

beings worthy of love and human contact. Provisions encouraged the infected to conduct responsible sexual relations and to disclose their status to potential partners. In addition, the men asserted the right of PWAs to have a voice in the development of policy for their care. The Denver Principles stated that the infected did not deserve blame for the syndrome. They also set forth the conditions they expected for their medical needs, including the right to unbiased service, the right to determine their course of treatment, the right to medical privacy, and the right to be surrounded by their chosen loved ones. Michael Callen read the final principle to an audience dissolving into tears.

People with AIDS had the right, said Callen, "To die—and to LIVE—in dignity."

PART TWO
CATASTROPHE
1983–1992

ONE
AIDS
DEATH
EVERY
THIRTY
MINUTES

ONE DAY THAN THE
IN EIGHT YEARS.

ACT UP poster, circa 1989.

"Someday, the AIDS crisis will be over. Remember that. And when that day comes . . . there will be people alive on this earth . . . who will hear the story that once there was a terrible disease in this country, and all over the world, and that a brave group of people stood up and fought and, in some cases, gave their lives, so that other people might live and be free."   —Vito Russo, 1988

CHAPTER 5

OUTED

1983–1985

IT didn't take long for Larry Kramer to lose more friends. Seven months after authoring his warning for the *Native*, Kramer purchased a full-page advertisement in New York's *Village Voice*. Plastered across his lengthy text was a banner that emphasized the escalating rate of infection: "2,339 and counting." Deaths were mounting, too, he reported. His first notice had listed the twenty people he'd known and lost to AIDS; the new one recognized ten more.

Despite Kramer's efforts to arouse awareness, many gay men continued to ignore his concerns. Some dismissed them as just another *Faggots*-style prudish characterization of gay sexuality. Some regarded AIDS as the latest effort by Americans to portray homosexuals in a negative light. Others feared that calling attention to a gay health emergency would undermine the ongoing quest for rights and political influence by what was still a heavily stigmatized community.

And not everyone shared Kramer's wealth of connections. Their friends weren't dying, so why be concerned? The outbreak seemed unlikely to touch them. In the earliest years, even for those living at its epicenters, AIDS could seem to be over there, infecting someone else. Infecting just a few individuals. Not friends. Not lovers. Not oneself. But then, in a sort of malicious reversal of expanding ripples, the circles of connection began to draw closer. The names of PWAs were no longer just names.

The names came with faces.

After people began recognizing their own friends and acquaintances among the dead and dying, AIDS became a topic of increasingly fearful discussion within gay communities in coastal hubs like San Francisco, Los Angeles, and New York. Who had it. Who might. Who knew someone that had been infected. What the hell could be causing it. What in heaven could be done to stop it. Individuals who were most concerned began responding to fund-raising appeals from within the gay community and started volunteering to help PWAs through New York's GMHC and San Francisco's Shanti Project.

Even those on the sidelines couldn't totally ignore the expanding web of infection. They looked beyond the old metrics of beauty and sex appeal and began scanning others for the telltale blemishes of KS and for signs of physical wasting. An acquaintance at a local gym might mysteriously disappear for a few weeks and then return visibly altered, almost undoubtedly having done battle with whatever was causing AIDS. Men still sought refuge on Fire Island, but the specter of death followed them there, too. "Suddenly it was common to see former stars of the beach bumping down the boardwalks in wheelchairs or tapping along with the aid of white canes," Steve Bolerjack wrote years later about his experience of living in New York during the AIDS crisis.

Fear grew among gay men after it became evident that symptoms of infection could take years to appear. For those who had been sexually promiscuous during the 1970s and early 1980s, the likelihood of having unwittingly contracted AIDS seemed almost inevitable. Only the moment of infection remained a matter of speculation. Later on, researchers would conclude that by 1983 at least half of all gay men living in New York and San Francisco had already contracted the virus that caused AIDS; they just hadn't known it because they hadn't become symptomatic. Even without the benefit of this scientific knowledge, thousands of gay men began to convert from an *if* mindset to one of *when*.

"Essentially, we did two things," Bolerjack wrote in 2001. "[We] watched helplessly as everyone around us fell, and then wondered how long we could remain standing." Fellow New Yorker Sean Strub recalled in his memoir *Body Counts* how, during those early years, "When I heard of someone who was sick, an instant Venn diagram appeared in my head, reflexively sketching out the sexual relationships that might connect me to that person."

AIDS shattered all prior realities. Even innocent inquiries about mutual acquaintances became risky. Too often the answers were grim. People grew accustomed to—and even obsessed with—scanning newspaper obituaries in case there were any familiar names. And they got adept at reading between the lines of the listed causes of death. *He died of cancer*, and *he died after a long illness*, and *he died from pneumonia* were coded phrases. They substituted for a truth some individuals or their survivors were not yet ready to face.

He died from AIDS.

It became a surreal experience for young men in their twenties and thirties to encounter so many reports of death among their peers—and to anticipate the possibility of their own. As more and more friends and acquaintances fell ill, it was perversely reassuring to bump into someone. Seeing was believing. Seeing meant the person wasn't dead. At least not yet.

If Americans living beyond the epicenters of infection ever heard of or thought about AIDS, they probably considered it an abstract illness that was unlikely to affect them. President Reagan and others in his administration continued to ignore the crisis despite its

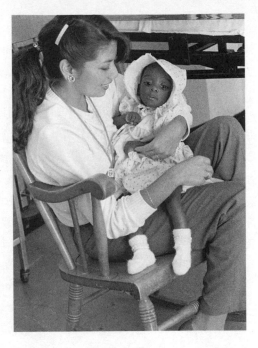

Healthcare worker Delia Cano nurtures an unidentified HIV-positive child in Miami, Florida, November 8, 1983. The fourteen-month-old girl's mother died from AIDS, and her father abandoned his infected child.

spreading reach, and White House officials excluded AIDS from subjects worthy of government attention. Surgeon General C. Everett Koop, the nation's top medical officer, held responsibility for addressing national health concerns, but he remained mute because his conservative supervisor had instructed him that he "would not be assigned to cover AIDS." The Republican-controlled Senate worked in concert with Reagan's administration, and Congress provided only modest additional appropriations to study the outbreak.

In places where the lives of PWAs intersected with people at lower risk of infection, such as New York City, concerns did rise. After a staffer at a Wall Street firm revealed he had AIDS, a panicked colleague sought advice by phoning St. Vincent's Hospital, which treated local PWAs. "Everybody is hysterical," the caller told physician Joyce Wallace. "Other people don't want to work with him. How do we protect ourselves?" The doctor's advice, based on the best scientific guesses by 1983, was straightforward and accurate. "Don't sleep with him, and don't share a needle with him."

People who worked in high-risk careers worried, too. Could female models share makeup brushes with gay male stylists? Could delivery people safely handle parcels and letters that referenced AIDS in the mailing address? What about hospital staffers delivering meals to the rooms of PWAs? Was it safe to stand near a gay colleague with a cough or to visit gay neighborhoods in lower Manhattan? Was it safe to hire a Haitian maid?

"Any homosexual or Haitian has become an object of dread," reported Michael Daly in a 1983 *New York* magazine article on "AIDS Anxiety." People worried about the health risks of riding New York City's subways, of attending religious services with gay men, even of swimming in communal pools—resurrecting a fear from the polio epidemic of earlier decades. Many of the concerns were without merit, but, without clear facts, anxieties grew. Some hospitals even turned away PWAs for fear that individuals with other illnesses would shun their facilities if they knew they treated AIDS patients.

Rumors abounded as the crisis grew. Many of them took decades to dispel. Meanwhile people disputed evidence about the source of infection; repeated a conspiracy theory of AIDS being a government-sponsored germ warfare attack on gay men; accused one man, a flight attendant named Gaëtan Dugas (who came to be known as "Patient Zero"), of having single-handedly spread the contagion through widespread promiscuity; and entertained other false but persistent claims.

▲

By the fall of 1983, researchers were increasingly sure they'd found the cause of the contagion. It took years of subsequent debate to name the lethal pathogen, and it took longer still to decide who deserved credit for its discovery, but eventually scientists settled on the name HIV, short for human immunodeficiency virus. Twenty-five years later Luc Montagnier and fellow scientist Françoise Barré-Sinoussi from the Pasteur Institute in Paris were awarded a Nobel Prize in Medicine for their leadership role in the historic discovery. Many also credit Robert Gallo and his team at the National Institutes of Health, but the Nobel Foundation did not commemorate their work.

The identification of HIV helped to confirm that the virus spread through contact with an infected person's blood or semen. The fact that someone could carry the virus for months or years without exhibiting symptoms made its containment problematic. Carriers could unwittingly pass the virus to others before realizing they were themselves ill. Healthcare workers began wearing protective gloves during every medical procedure for their own security and for the safety of their patients—a major change in doctor and dental offices where bare hands had been the norm—and researchers rushed to develop a test to detect the virus in people who otherwise seemed to be healthy.

Such tests appeared in 1984 and were in widespread use the following year. In addition to identifying the presence of HIV among individuals, the new tests finally made it possible to start purging the virus from the nation's stockpiles of human blood. By then, however, contaminated donations had infected many others, particularly hemophiliacs. The United States had even contributed to the international spread of AIDS among hemophiliacs because American firms supplied essential clotting products to much of the world. In some countries more than half of all hemophiliacs had been infected with HIV prior to proper screening in 1985. Such transmissions helped transform what had begun as a regional epidemic into a worldwide pandemic.

In November 1984 Ronald Reagan won reelection without having ever publicly uttered the word AIDS or even commenting on the health crisis that had built throughout his first term in office. More than 5,500 Americans had died because of the syndrome during this four-year period, and over 7,000 were living with AIDS when he began his second term. "Is the president concerned about this subject?" Lester Kinsolving had kept asking during White House press briefings, but Reagan's press secretary dismissed the journalist's ongoing interest with evasive answers and homophobic teasing that routinely drew laughs from other reporters in the press room.

All that changed on July 25, 1985.

On that day, a news bombshell broke through the indifference of the press corps, the Reagan administration, members of Congress, and citizens at large. Hollywood heartthrob Rock Hudson was gravely ill. And not just with any illness. Hudson had AIDS. Widely known for his roles as one of cinema's iconic romantic stars, Hudson was a handsome and popular actor. The shocking stories about his illness also revealed that everyone's favorite leading man had been living a deeply closeted life. Any one of the three disclosures—Hudson being gay, dangerously sick, and afflicted with AIDS—would have snapped heads to attention. The triple whammy riveted the nation, and almost overnight Americans began to think differently about the syndrome.

If Rock Hudson could get AIDS, anyone could.

Americans followed breaking news updates about Hudson's fight for survival, including his return journey by private plane from France where he had gone in search of experimental treatment. The news of Rock Hudson's health battles didn't just capture the country's attention; it touched President Reagan personally. Perhaps for the first time he knew someone with AIDS. He and his wife, Nancy Reagan, weren't just fans of Hudson's films. They'd known the man personally from their earlier careers as Hollywood actors. Hudson had even been their guest at the White House.

Two months after learning of his friend's infection, and more than four and a half years after assuming the presidency, Reagan broke his silence over AIDS. During a press conference on September 17, 1985, he responded to a question about federal funding for the study of the syndrome. He defended his administration's commitment to

Left: Rock Hudson with Nancy and Ronald Reagan during a White House State Dinner, May 15, 1984. Below: Hudson with actress Doris Day, July 18, 1985. The effects of HIV had ravaged his physical appearance in just over one year.

research and described it as "one of the top priorities" of his presidency, a claim unsupported by the historical record. Later that year Congress took action on its own and began to allocate increasingly significant sums of money for medical research on HIV and AIDS. These efforts didn't help Hudson—he died from his infection that October at age fifty-nine—but they at least marked a turning point in the fight against it.

By then the nation's previous not-my-problem attitude had created dire consequences. Between 1981 and 1984, the syndrome accounted for the deaths of an estimated 5,663 people in the United States. In 1985, the number of AIDS-related deaths was 6,996. In the span of a single year, AIDS had claimed the lives of more people than in the previous four. Combined. A more assertive federal response might have blunted the spread of infection and increased the possibility of its containment. Instead the nation experienced a vastly more serious and enduring crisis.

AIDS became a catastrophe.

CHAPTER 6

POSITIVE

"NOW no one is safe from AIDS," the headline on a *LIFE* magazine cover noted in July 1985. Accompanying articles focused on what were called "the new victims" of AIDS, the people who were being drawn into the crisis because "the AIDS minorities are beginning to infect the heterosexual, drug-free majority." Yet even as AIDS spread to ever more people, few rallied to support them. When a story broke the next month about thirteen-year-old HIV-positive Ryan White, many condoned his Indiana school district's decision to exclude him from attending classes. White, a hemophiliac, had developed AIDS following a routine transfusion, and his legal fight to return to the classroom ignited a national debate about the rights of a PWA versus the risks of exposure faced by someone who might interact with them.

White's situation may not have prompted an outpouring of sympathy, but stories like his and Rock Hudson's did capture the public's attention. Media coverage reinforced how much remained unknown about the syndrome; scientists were barely starting to make sense of it. Everyone who contracted AIDS died, and considerable misinformation circulated about what caused it and how to contain its spread. In the face of such uncertainty, people pursued the next logical alternative.

They panicked.

Millions of Americans who had previously ignored AIDS suddenly became anxious about becoming infected, and they began identifying points of potential contagion, with or without the use of scientific evidence. Rumors swirled. Seemingly the AIDS virus could be anywhere.

On toilet seats in public bathrooms.

In the comingling of blood from mosquito bites.

On the utensils and dishes used by infected people.

There was no factual basis for these fears, but that didn't stop people from purchasing travel packs of toilet seat covers (free public dispensers had not yet become commonplace). It didn't prevent people from worrying after receiving mosquito bites. And it didn't stop family members and friends from withholding hugs from PWAs and giving them disposable utensils and dishes at shared meals, assuming they still shared meals at all.

The federal government had done so little to educate the public about HIV and AIDS that gay men were increasingly targeted in hate crimes. AIDS-based discrimination became yet another part of the health crisis. In addition to the risks of being fired and evicted, PWAs found it hard to obtain health insurance at a time when they most needed it. Medical personnel might deny them services, such as mouth-to-mouth resuscitation.

An Alaska Department of Health AIDS Prevention Project poster from the 1980s.

Funeral homes might refuse to handle their remains after their deaths.

The syndrome acquired an undeserved but almost permanent stigma. That stigma started by being associated with the marginalized communities of gay men and drug users. It spread through unfounded fears of contagion. It grew because of a general discomfort with discussing intimate matters of sexual intercourse. And it blossomed during a conservative era that brought and kept President Reagan in office. Many Americans believed AIDS to be an illness that afflicted people who must have done something wrong. Even when they had contracted the virus through a blood product—as was the case with Ryan White—the stigma remained. This mindset made it that much harder to promote the civil rights of PWAs and to develop strategies for curtailing the spread of HIV.

Conservative religious leaders and members of Congress argued against prevention proposals for distributing condoms and establishing needle exchanges. Giving away condoms made it look like the government was promoting promiscuity, they argued. And exchanges that allowed addicts to swap used needles for clean ones seemed like an endorsement of illegal drug use at a time when substance abuse was becoming its own health crisis. Advocates argued that it was immoral to allow AIDS to continue to spread, and that studies failed to support claims that promiscuity and drug use would increase under such programs. When the federal government refused to fund needle exchanges as a harm reduction strategy, a limited number of local governments and so-

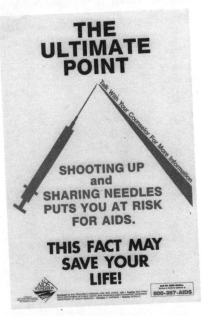

A San Francisco Forensic AIDS Task Force poster, 1985.

cial service organizations began to fill the gap, but their success was inevitably less impactful than a nationwide campaign.

▲

Starting in 1985, the ability to test for HIV raised a conundrum for gay men and those in other high-risk groups. What should they do? Test? Or not test? Was it better to know one faced an incurable condition and certain death, or was it preferable to retain some sense of innocence and hope? Why bother being tested if no treatment existed for the condition and a positive result could lead to negative consequences? Why risk it when the admission of being positive carried such stigma?

Even being tested and coming up negative had drawbacks. Did it seem boastful to reveal the confirmation of not being infected? Did it suggest having feared the opposite outcome because of past behaviors? Wouldn't that implication just create stigma, too? Would coming up negative create barriers in relationships? Would the once-unifying force of shared gay identity cleave into two parts, segregated by simple mathematical symbols, the plus sign or the minus mark?

The earliest tests were not particularly accurate—issuing results with false positives and negatives—and their unreliability made it easy for some to dismiss the idea of testing altogether. Others resisted it while they remained free of symptoms—although after they arrived one hardly needed a test, particularly if HIV marked its presence through the appearance of darkened red and purple KS lesions. With or without testing, apprehension mounted. "Everybody was fearful," Steve Bolerjack recalled. "If we weren't sick, we were afraid we would be. If we weren't HIV-positive, we were afraid it was just a matter of time."

Testing almost inevitably meant interacting with doctors, a complicated prospect for gay men who remembered how the

Mourners honor people who died from AIDS at a candlelight vigil in San Jose, California, 1985. Such ceremonies were held across the country throughout the 1980s and beyond.

medical establishment had previously classified homosexuality as a mental illness. The repudiation of that stance in 1973 had freed gay doctors to come out of the closet, and many of these physicians became part of the front lines in the fight against HIV through practices they'd established to serve the gay community. Not all physicians were as welcoming. Some refused to treat PWAs until the American Medical Association required them to provide care without discrimination.

For those who sought testing, positive results generally came with a physician's prediction of life expectancies. These estimates varied depending on the person's state of health.

You have six weeks to live.

You might last six months.

You should have two good years left.

Without any known course of treatment, few physicians promised more than two years. The best advice they had for PWAs was to stay healthy. It could be difficult to recover from opportunistic infections such as pneumonia, they warned, a fact that those living at the epicenters of infection knew firsthand after watching friends and others die because of them. They'd seen how hard it could be to earn a second chance at survival.

People tested for HIV today are classified as being either HIV-positive or HIV-negative. A positive test means HIV antibodies have developed in the blood, a process known as seroconversion that happens soon after infection. People may talk about their sero status being positive or negative. But in 1985, there was no such vocabulary. People who tested positive only had one sentence to convey their situation: *I have AIDS*.

Over time a vocabulary began to grow and evolve. Medical professionals initially described people who carried the virus as having AIDS-related complex, or ARC, and they classified those with end-stage symptoms as exhibiting full-blown AIDS. As appreciation grew over the range of difference between HIV as an infection and AIDS as a terminal illness, the name for the syndrome changed. HIV-positive individuals are said to have AIDS only if they contract opportunistic infections or exhibit other life-threatening symptoms of the syndrome. The stages along this continuum—from sero-conversion to living with infection to being at risk of death—are collectively referred to as HIV/AIDS.

▲

News of an HIV-positive diagnosis landed hard in those early years when there was no hope for treatment. "When I left [the doctor's] office, I was in a daze," Strub wrote in his memoir. "My head felt like it was floating, and I found it impossible to concentrate. Everything was different, but I wasn't ready to face my new reality."

"At the time I was diagnosed," champion diver Greg Louganis

said, "we thought of HIV as a death sentence. It was six months prior to the Olympic Games, and I was like, 'Well, I'm going to pack my bags and go home and lock myself in my house and wait to die.'"

"I didn't want to believe him," basketball star Earvin "Magic" Johnson recalled thinking when the Lakers team physician told him he'd come up HIV-positive during a routine blood test. He thought immediately of his wife and their unborn child, fearing that he might have unwittingly spread the infection to them, but further testing soon confirmed that he had not.

Doris Butler had contracted HIV through intravenous drug use. Later she learned that she had passed the infection on to her infant child. When she tried to recall her reaction to this news for documentary filmmaker Peter Adair some time afterward, she could hardly find words for her feelings. "When I think about that particular moment, it really hurts a whole bunch," she finally said, speaking through tears.

Adair, who was likewise HIV-positive, told viewers of his film *Absolutely Positive* that "I'm having trouble accepting that HIV is now a part of who I am. Growing up, misfortune was always over there. Those poor starving people in India. . . . But now it's not over there. It's in here."

Jonnie Norway told Adair about his reaction to testing positive. "You find out this information and you're crushed. You crumble. And then you talk to people and kinda put yourself back together. And once you're kinda, sorta put back together, that's when you get courage."

Courage was a good thing. Courage became another essential element of the fight against AIDS, right up there with Michael Callen's hope, Dan Turner's optimism, and Bobbi Campbell's outreach.

People would need all four and more to face AIDS.

CHAPTER 7

TRANSITIONS

1985–1986

AFTER Bobbi Campbell had helped to found People with AIDS in Denver during the summer of 1983, he had continued his Poster Boy awareness campaign by traveling and speaking at events around the country. His efforts undoubtedly improved and even saved the lives of others, but they didn't bring results in time to save his own. Campbell died from AIDS on August 15, 1984, after a three-year fight, at the age of thirty-two.

So it went in the opening years of the epidemic. Some people died with breathtaking haste, especially in the beginning. Julie Rhoad, a Broadway stage manager at the time, recalled how "you watched people die rapid, hard deaths. There one week, gone the next. You never knew who would show up to perform on any given night."

"People would go fast," New York artist Kenny Scharf told a journalist in 2017. "One minute they were a beautiful 20-year-old, the next you could see the look of death in their face." AIDS historian David France described a coworker in New York who stayed out late on a Thursday night to attend a concert. "Friday he had a fever. Sunday he was hospitalized. Wednesday he was dead."

People whose lives had barely begun found themselves facing their imminent demise. "I can't do a lot of things anymore," twenty-two-year-old Todd Coleman observed in 1985. Coleman had moved from Denver to San Francisco when he was sixteen. By twenty-one he was symptomatic with AIDS. "I feel like an elderly person in a room and weak, getting my social security. Old people and I have a lot in common," he told filmmaker Tina DiFeliciantonio in *Living with AIDS*. When asked what he would request of others, he replied, "Just don't turn away from us all, 'cause a lot of kids, a lot of men need help." He added, "I don't want to see any other twenty-two-year-old go through this; I really don't." Coleman died six weeks later.

"It's a hideous disease," Jerry Smith told a *Washington Post* reporter in 1986. Smith had been a celebrated tight end for the Washington Redskins at the time of his 1978 retirement, but in 1986, at age forty-three, he lay dying of AIDS. Smith declined to discuss the source of his infection but noted, "I'm angry for myself, and I'm angry because I don't want anybody to have to go through this."

Being HIV-positive required endless decisions, including the question of how widely to share the news—or whether to reveal it at all. There were wills to write. There was work to face in hopes of staying insured and financially solvent. And there were relationships to navigate.

With friends.

With family.

With lovers.

With strangers.

Sexual relations were particularly problematic. Did being HIV-positive mean giving up all sex? Or just certain sexual acts? Or only having sex with another positive person? Or only having sex using condoms? Was being HIV-positive something that a person had to

Workers offer advice on how to prevent HIV infection, Southern California, June 22, 1986. Local campaigns provided safe sex education during the early years of the epidemic when the federal government remained disengaged from prevention efforts.

divulge before engaging in sex with someone for the first time? Even strangers? It wasn't exactly a compelling pick-up line.

HIV hit the United States at a time when many gay men continued to live binary lives—out to other gays but closeted to everyone else. Relationships with family members, friends, and employers might unfold through a web of filtered information. HIV blew that system apart. Frequently men found themselves forced to disclose two secrets at once: being gay and being HIV-positive. Responses ranged from acceptance to complete rejection, including immediate dismissal from work. Some men never shared their secrets. Bosses, coworkers, friends, and relatives might only find out after a person was gone that he had been gay, that he had had AIDS—if they found out at all.

The stigma of coming out as HIV-positive was no less severe for intravenous drug users, or people who had intercourse with those drug users but weren't addicts themselves. Even people infected through contaminated blood felt shame, felt somehow marked by HIV. "Well, gee, did I, do I really deserve this?" Margery Middleton found herself thinking, having contracted the virus through intercourse with her husband, who had been infected by a blood transfusion.

Amidst the fear, stigma, and despair each person had to navigate how to keep living. Many HIV-positive people sold property and cashed in life insurance policies to create extra financial liquidity. Some saved the money for medical emergencies. Others blew it on the trips they'd always intended to take someday. That day was now, they figured. Few made long-term plans. What was the point?

And yet the knowledge of a terminal illness could breathe fresh meaning into the everyday and inspire people to tackle surprisingly large challenges. Sean Strub went on to found *POZ*, a magazine dedicated to helping people live with being HIV-positive. Greg Louganis chose to compete in the 1988 Olympics after all; he won two gold medals in Seoul, Korea, despite hitting his head on the diving board during one of his complex maneuvers. And Peter Adair stuck with filmmaking.

"How do you live in a room with a monster?" Adair asked rhetorically during *Absolutely Positive*. "How do you just go about your life? I tried denying his presence, but I kept bumping into the beast. And now that I fully admit he's here, I worry I'll become obsessed, jumping at his every twitch and move. Is there a balance between denial and obsession? The only answer is to coexist with this monster, [to] learn how to eat out of the same bowl."

Those living with HIV became adept at reading their bodies' signs. If they were tired, they rested. If a certain food disagreed with them, they stopped eating it. Many explored alternative therapies like vitamin regimens, unapproved drugs that were smuggled into the United States, exotic treatments hawked by charlatans, dietary fads, meditation, religion, visualization, crystal therapy, and on, and on, and on.

But self-care regimens brought their own pressures. In *Absolutely Positive* Gregg Cassin explained how hard it could be to stay forward-thinking and upbeat: "I've always got to be spiritual. I've always got to be happy. I've always got to be aware. I've got to be expanded. I've got to be healing myself. I can't be getting sicker. I can't be blah, blah, blah." Cassin told Adair that he had decided to change his approach. "My new goal is to be human," he said. "It's my right to have a shitty day. It's my right to have a cold; I'm a human being. It's my right to be a bitch. It's my right to be less than perfect. It's my right to be HIV-positive. Even there, I can be loved even there. Even in something that my mind or this world has said is so ugly, but I can find a place to be gentle and compassionate with that and to love that."

When compassion, and positive thinking, and all other strategies failed to keep the opportunistic infections at bay, hospitalization became the next line of defense. Some medical centers, especially those at the epicenters of infection in New York City and San Francisco, had entire wards dedicated to the care of PWAs. Sometimes physicians and nurses were able to stabilize patients long enough for their immune systems to mount a comeback and earn a reprieve. That second chance at survival.

In New York City, St. Vincent's Hospital became increasingly devoted to the care of PWAs, in part because it was located in Greenwich Village near where many gay men lived. "By 1986, a third of the hospital's beds were filled by AIDS patients," recalled *New Yorker* writer Andrew Boynton in a retrospective tribute to the facility. "St. Vincent's soon became ground zero in the city's AIDS crisis." Friends and lovers sometimes went to visit one person only to recognize other names on hospital room doors. "Several times, I went to the AIDS ward at St. Vincent's Hospital without intending to visit

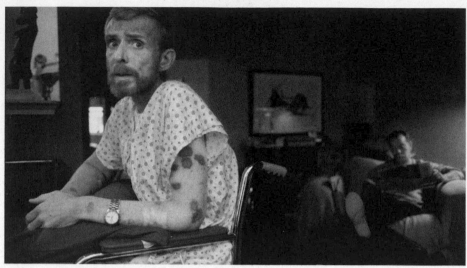

KS lesions cover the body of Ken Meeks, September 1986. Meeks, a member of the GMHC board, died three days after this photograph was taken. He was forty-five years old. The image, published soon after in LIFE magazine, became an iconic representation of the human face of HIV/AIDS.

anyone in particular," Sean Strub recalled in his memoir, "knowing there would be someone I knew who was there."

When second chances didn't come—and often they did not—individuals considered the inevitable. "Steven, I have always loved you and, if there is some survival beyond death, I always shall," Bruce Philip Cooper wrote to his lover in 1986 as his life drew to a close. "More than anything, I regret that we shall not grow old together. More than anything, I hope that we shall meet again beyond death." Cooper died the next year; his partner's death followed eight years later.

Healthcare workers, friends, and loved ones became familiar with the realities of what it meant to watch someone die from AIDS. They learned how to sit quietly when a loving presence was more comforting than conversation and how to become the keepers of last wishes. They witnessed horrifying physical disfiguration, unspeakable suffering, and wrenching partings.

They also glimpsed moments of grace. In his memoir, Strub recalled visiting Ken Dawson, a dying friend, former high school principal, and gay activist. Dawson, who had become too weak to leave his bed, asked his visitor, "Do you remember how we said we would want someone to pull the plug if we got terribly ill?" Strub did remember. Dawson continued, slowly, "Well, I am way past the point where I would have thought I wanted to die . . . Wa-a-a-y past it." But then he commented on his pleasure at seeing his friend, and even of observing something as simple as the sunshine that lit a wall of his room. "I never thought I could be so sick and yet still have such a nice day." During an era of constant suffering and death, Strub observed, "We personally witnessed the courage and grace of loved ones in their effort to be alive for their deaths."

And then they were gone.

Some died naturally, the outcome of the unnatural effects of HIV. Others took their own lives. At times friends gathered to keep vigil or assist during the appointed hours of suicides. At others they only heard afterward of the taking of a life. "By the time you receive this letter, unless something goes terribly wrong, I will be dead," one man wrote in a notice he mailed to selected family members and friends. "Instead of grieving for me, please be happy that I was able to be in charge of my final days."

Funerals became the new normal. "We were going to more funerals and memorial services than birthday parties," Strub recalled about the early years of the epidemic. "And you didn't even have time to grieve because you were so quickly on to the next death." Reactions varied when family members were hit with a trifecta of revelations: the death of a relative, the fact that he'd died from AIDS, and his identity as a gay man. Some accepted the news and welcomed the discovery of gay friends and partners. "When you are sitting close to me, I feel like I am so much closer to my Michael," a mother told Strub at the memorial service for the man who had been her son and his lover. Others claimed the deceased's physical remains but rejected his gay friends and lovers, throwing them out of shared living spaces, barring them from funerals, and cutting them off from financial legacies. Still others abandoned the dying altogether, leaving friends and partners to prepare a body for burial or make plans for scattering its ashes.

Grieving lovers clung to memories and even to articles of clothing that retained the scent of a lost partner. Grieving friends tallied the mounting losses, first individually and then by entire groups of people. The deaths of every summer resident from a shared house on Fire Island. The deaths of every person who had participated in a pre-AIDS gathering for group sex. The deaths of scores and then hundreds and eventually thousands of people who had marched during the annual gay pride parades that commemorated the 1969 Stonewall riots. By 1982, the fallen were themselves being commemorated during the annual marches.

Those who witnessed multiple deaths seemed almost instinctively to have made lists to remember the dead, as Larry Kramer had done when his friends began to die. Some wrote them down. Others annotated their address books to mark the losses. Some began data files on early personal computers. Others created art projects in memory of the dead or had names of the deceased printed onto articles of clothing. Still others saved the individual cards that they pulled from their loose-leaf Rolodexes of contact information. "That's my Rolo-dead file," one friend explained to Strub after he spotted a rubber-banded bundle of the paper tabs.

"I'm an organized person and when it all started," recalled Steve Bolerjack, "as people—friends, acquaintances, neighbors, gym buddies, work colleagues, activist colleagues—tested positive and became ill, I began a list. Then when they started dying, I began another list. It was a way to somehow try limiting an uncontrollable situation. I needed and wanted to remember them.

"But when that list got to be into dozens and dozens and then around a hundred," he said, "I stopped."

CHAPTER 8

OUTRAGE

1987

"IF my speech tonight doesn't scare the shit out of you, we're in trouble," said Larry Kramer, echoing the opening of his 1983 article in the *Native*. Speaking four years later on March 10, 1987, at the Lesbian and Gay Community Center in lower Manhattan, he continued: "I have never been able to understand why we have sat back and let ourselves literally be knocked off man by man without fighting back. I have heard of denial, but this is more than denial—it is a death wish." Yet again, Kramer threw down the gauntlet.

This time the LGBTQ community accepted the challenge.

Kramer's message landed at just the right moment. It caught the growing wave of fear, frustration, and outrage over an exponential toll of death. And it came with an indisputable target: the federal government and its sluggish drug approval process. "One of the top AIDS doctors in the United States can't get protocols through the FDA," Kramer said of the Food and Drug Administration. There were drugs out there, Kramer reported; they just couldn't get to market. It was time for political action, he urged.

Time for a fresh start.

Time to take action.

Time to act up.

Two days later, several hundred people who had either attended Kramer's speech or heard about it returned to the Lesbian and Gay Community Center to form the AIDS Coalition to Unleash Power, otherwise known as ACT UP. "I think I'm alive because of Larry Kramer and all the activists he led," Steve Bolerjack said in 2017. "The activism saved me and eventually many others."

Until the arrival of HIV, cooperative efforts between gay men and lesbians had been modest at best. They collaborated to a limited degree on pre- and post-Stonewall activism, but gender-aligned goals and interests largely pulled them in separate directions. After the 1986 Supreme Court decision *Bowers v. Hardwick*, which permitted states to continue criminalizing homosexual sex even between consenting adults, enraged members of the LGBTQ population began to work more closely together to obtain equal rights and fair treatment. Homophobia hurt everyone, they reasoned.

AIDS illustrated that point perfectly. The disregard most heterosexual people showed for dying gay men demonstrated an intrinsic bias against anyone who differed from perceived norms. If the gay community didn't challenge this discrimination, it could spread in ways that affected them all. The best antidote was action.

Lesbians, in a show of solidarity with their gay brothers, volunteered to help PWAs as caregivers, advocates, companions, and through their careers in healthcare. This infusion of female support, leadership, talent, and stamina emerged during the earliest years of the crisis through involvement in organizations like GMHC and as frontline nurses and doctors, and it grew as the crisis deepened. Women activists became essential in a fight where illness inevitably weakened and thinned the ranks of men. Women literally helped keep the movement going.

"Together, gay men and lesbians forged a very strong alliance

Marchers take part in a candlelight procession through West Hollywood, California, May 29, 1987. Some two thousand people walked to honor those who had died from AIDS.

that worked internally to support each other as friends and lovers died," ACT UP participant Alexis Danzig recalled in 2015. They also channeled their "mutual anger and outrage" into advocacy. This crisis-inspired collaboration helped dissolve past divides. Gay men became more sensitive to the political and cultural challenges faced by lesbians. Their shared experiences helped LGBTQ people weave the threads of past advocacy into an increasingly unified and effective activist community.

ACT UP was the embodiment of that evolution. It sprang from activist organizations that had been born in the wake of the Stonewall riots, from Fire Island's sense of liberation and solidarity, from the gay community's early responses to AIDS—*How to Have Sex in an Epidemic*, GMHC, the Denver Principles, and more. Virginia Apuzzo, the organizer who had helped foster the birth of the Principles, continued her advocacy through the National Gay

Task Force and a coalition of local service groups known as AIDS Action. Michael Callen, one of the Principles' authors, helped start the PWA Coalition to advocate for the HIV-positive; and GLAAD, the Gay and Lesbian Alliance Against Defamation, was founded to fight hate speech and violence directed at PWAs and others.

Just months before the founding of ACT UP, an activist named Marty Robinson revived the guerrilla theater–style "zaps" he'd helped organize during the post-Stonewall push for gay rights. Robinson formed a troupe of activists called the Lavender Hill Mob. Most of the group's attention-grabbing protests took place in New York, but in February 1987, he and other so-called Mobsters traveled to Atlanta to disrupt a CDC conference where the merits of mandatory HIV testing for hospital patients was under consideration. Such an idea raised fears of mass quarantines for the HIV-positive, and Robinson's group protested it by using the language of the Holocaust. Mobsters charged the Reagan administration with "Mass Murder by Indifference" and called the CDC the "Center for Detention Camps."

Two HIV-positive participants, Michael Petrelis and Eric Perez, wore homemade concentration camp–style uniforms. Their costumes included the pink triangle symbol that Nazis had used to identify homosexual prisoners. The pair debuted this attire at a preconference cocktail party and maintained an ominous presence at subsequent sessions. Such theatrics and the group's relentless calls throughout the meeting to "Test drugs, not people!" helped to defeat the mandatory testing initiative. Soon after Robinson, Petrelis, and other Mobsters became some of the founding members of ACT UP.

Several months earlier a poster had mysteriously begun appearing around New York City. Its origins were initially unknown, but its visual impact was irresistible. It used the same Nazi-era triangle Robinson's Mobsters had referenced: nestled in a vast field of inky blackness sat a neon-pink triangle, inverted so that it pointed up, not down. A stark equation sat below it, SILENCE = DEATH.

Silence equals death.

The poster was a call to action and contributed to the founding energy of ACT UP. "Being silent doesn't make the fear go away," activist Phil Wilson would later say. "In fact, being bold, speaking, helps us deal with the fear." The newly organized members of ACT UP took only two weeks to plan their first protest. They decided to stage their action on Wall Street, the heart of America's financial markets,

An anonymous arts collective launched this provocative poster in December, 1986, in an effort to spur action in the face of the epidemic. ACT UP formed soon after.

and they targeted the pharmaceutical industry, accusing it of being too slow in responding to the AIDS crisis.

Most researchers argued that such charges were unjustified. The field of virology was relatively new and HIV was so uniquely complex, they explained, that it had taken considerable time just to identify the virus and understand its weaknesses. Even then they had faced a steep challenge. Rapid mutations make viruses far trickier to outwit than bacteria. In the two decades before the arrival of HIV, scientists had successfully developed only five antiviral drugs of any kind. Even after identifying possible medications for combating HIV, drug makers needed to follow the FDA's strict medication approval process, a painstaking system of comparative testing that sought to protect the public from dangerous side effects. Researchers measured the six years since the arrival of AIDS by the considerable advancements they'd made using cutting-edge science. Activists measured the same period by the loss of 25,000 people.

▲

On March 19, 1987, five days before ACT UP's debut action, the nation's first medication for the treatment of people with AIDS—a drug commonly referred to as AZT—entered the marketplace. AZT was not actually a new drug. Federal researchers using taxpayer money had synthesized it years earlier in hopes of combating viral cancers, but it had failed to work. In 1985 Burroughs Wellcome, the pharmaceutical company that held the medication's patent, had authorized federal labs to begin testing whether it might control the spread of HIV. A second round of testing in the fall of 1986 had shown that people taking AZT lived longer than those who received a placebo, so Burroughs Wellcome received FDA approval to manufacture and sell the drug.

The arrival of AZT had been widely anticipated, but no one was prepared for its accompanying price tag, an eye-popping $10,000 per year, per person (equivalent to about twice that amount in today's dollars). During the drug's lengthy approval process Burroughs Wellcome had provided AZT at no charge to PWAs. But when the firm gained permission to start selling the medication, anyone who had been receiving it for free suddenly had to pay thousands of dollars to continue therapy. Many simply could not afford it. As a further insult, taxpayer-funded federal research had brought the drug to market, yet a single private company would benefit from astronomical profits.

So when ACT UP took to Wall Street on March 24, 1987, frustrations over the government's lethargic drug approval process and fury over the new AZT prices gave protesters plenty of reasons to, as one sign said, "Turn fear into rage." Activists blocked traffic for hours, shouted, made noise, handed out leaflets, and hung the commissioner of the FDA in effigy. Police arrested seventeen people in the full glare of the news media spotlight. Shortly after the demonstration, the FDA announced that it would begin streamlining drug testing procedures, shaving two years off what nonetheless continued to be a slow and complicated process.

ACT UP kept protesting AZT pricing with dramatic demonstrations against Burroughs Wellcome at its North Carolina headquarters and on the floor of the New York Stock Exchange. Public outcry became so intense that the company reduced the medication's annual cost to about $6,500. The price remained prohibitively expensive for many people, particularly those who were too ill to work and had lost their employer-based health insurance. Congress enacted an emergency federal assistance program to help support the truly impoverished, but plenty of people fell through the cracks and failed to receive treatment.

In time it became clear that AZT wasn't the miracle drug people had first hoped. At best, it seemed to prolong someone's life by a few weeks or months. It turned out that AZT worked only as long as it took the virus to mutate and outsmart the drug's chemistry. Increased doses just exacerbated its toxic side effects. If AIDS didn't kill a person, AZT probably would. Activist Michael Callen dismissed the drug as Drano, the poisonous drain-cleaning product. As its drawbacks became apparent, some avoided it entirely or discontinued their use of it, especially if they were not yet experiencing opportunistic infections and other end-stage symptoms of AIDS. Later, many would credit this decision with saving their lives.

▲

ACT UP's opening protests were evidence of the monumental energy and considerable talent within the organization. From its base in New York City it could call on some of the nation's most capable forces in marketing, public relations, management, theater, graphic design, and more. A collective of six gay artists came out of the shadows at an early ACT UP meeting and admitted to creating the SILENCE = DEATH poster. They shared their logo and slogan with the group and signed on to create further materials, working under the name Gran Fury.

Not everyone who joined ACT UP's efforts was HIV-positive or even gay. The cause attracted straight allies, the young and old, people of diverse backgrounds—anyone fired up and ready to fight AIDS, or as participants chanted repeatedly, anyone ready to *Act up! Fight back! Fight AIDS!*

Women assumed key leadership roles in the organization. Ann Northrop, a savvy former CBS news producer, helped to sculpt the organization's message. "You don't speak *to* the media," Sean Strub remembers learning from Northrop. "You speak *through* the media." Amy Bauer was a key instructor in the tactics of nonviolent civil disobedience, skills she'd acquired through years of work as a peace activist. She taught members how to interact with law enforcement officers, including during provocative protests that were designed to spark arrests. Maxine Wolfe, a college professor and longtime activist, brought organizational skills to ACT UP, helped to facilitate meetings, and advocated on behalf of women living with HIV/AIDS.

ACT UP members met every Monday evening in sessions that could last for hours. The organization was structured yet creatively fluid. Every meeting started by reading the names of recently deceased members and friends and by repeating the ACT UP mission: "We are a diverse, non-partisan group of individuals united in anger and committed to direct action to end the AIDS crisis," the statement began. Over time, its subsequent text was distilled into three pithy declarations:

We advise and inform.

We demonstrate.

We are not silent.

After that participants planned, shared updates, trained, taught, flirted, told stories, laughed, fumed, cried, and did whatever else was required to support a movement for social change.

"Everything ACT UP did it did analog," recalled Garance Franke-Ruta, who became involved with ACT UP when she was seventeen. "It posted posters on actual walls, with wheat-paste mixed in great buckets and slapped up late at night by members risking arrest. People spread messages through phone trees, from their landlines," she noted in a 2013 remembrance of the organization. She added: "ACT UP believed in training. It believed in planning, logistics, tactics, strategy, clearly articulated and well-researched demands, and, most importantly, it believed in getting results."

Each weekly meeting ended with the signature chant: *Act up! Fight back! Fight AIDS!*

Chants became an essential weapon for the organization. They infused the group with a sort of primal energy, just as chanting and singing had done during the civil rights movement. Sharing the same verses or phrases built unity, combated individual fears, and fed the collective power.

ACT UP member Ron Goldberg took the lead on creating and teaching new chants. He deliberately constructed phrases with irresistible rhythms and intuitive spaces for taking breaths. Often the chants employed biting wit. Some, as had been the case with the protest songs of earlier movements, could be adapted to suit the needs of a particular action; just substitute a word or phrase, and an old chant would fit a new occasion.

Many chants worked in the call-and-response style. A leader

with a megaphone could shout *we die* and trigger a massive response of *they do nothing!* Or groups could take turns chanting. One segment would ask, *People with AIDS, under attack. What do we do?* The answer became, *Act up! Fight back!* Activists transformed straightforward statements—*Healthcare is a right*—into commanding chants through the use of strategic syncopation: *Health* (pause) *care* (pause) *is a right; healthcare is a right.* Another chant employed similar pauses after the first two words, *No more business as usual.*

The media-savvy Ann Northrop drilled participants so that anyone could serve as an ACT UP spokesperson. Goldberg's chants often became made-to-order sound bites for television news. As he recalled in 2016, "If they stuck a microphone in your face and asked, 'Well, why are you here?' You would answer 'Because healthcare is a right!'"

Amy Bauer coached protesters on the use of civil disobedience tactics. Activists learned to collectively shout a warning to the authorities—*no violence, no violence*—when police officers stepped forward to arrest or otherwise interact with protesters. The chant reminded officers that they had no right to mistreat people who were protesting peacefully, even if they were protesting with considerable effect and noise. It helped keep tense protests from deteriorating into violent confrontations.

Many ACT UP members adopted a provocative look. In contrast to the nonthreatening, we-are-just-like-you business attire chosen by advocates for gay rights during the 1960s, these warriors selected more battle-worthy clothing. Key items included black combat-style boots, white T-shirts under black leather bomber jackets, and, as AIDS historian David France has described them, "jeans tight as a sunburn."

The chanting, the bodies in the street, ceaseless creativity, and an ever-present neon-pink triangle all became part of an un-

A syndicated political cartoon by Ed Gamble of the Florida Times-Union, *1987. Funding for HIV/AIDS research remained insufficient during the Reagan administration, enraging activists and sparking repeated protests.*

stoppable ACT UP force. "It was my life," said filmmaker Gregg Bordowitz, recalling the period from 1987 to 1993 when his efforts included preparing members for acts of civil disobedience. "It was all I did. Every meaningful relationship I had was with people who were in ACT UP. There was nothing else outside of it."

Affinity groups sprang up within the organization, small teams of participants who tackled specific assignments. These semi-autonomous units often met for additional activities beyond the weekly ACT UP meetings. Potluck suppers. Practice sessions. Strategic planning. Each group contributed its energy and creativity to the whole. One affinity group named Wave 3 featured twenty activists who specialized in being arrested; they practiced a form of civil disobedience that required training, courage, and a willingness to acquire a police record.

Bordowitz and others with experience in filmmaking formed

DIVA TV, short for Damned Interfering Video Activist Television. DIVA TV crews didn't just record archival footage of what the activists did. They documented what was done to them, similar to the way cell phone cameras are used in the twenty-first century. When a police officer erroneously charged a protestor with assault, DIVA TV footage offered undeniable evidence to the contrary. When an officer claimed someone had brought a firecracker to a protest, DIVA TV showed that the officer had actually tainted the evidence by sneaking the illegal explosive into the person's confiscated belongings.

Seven months after its founding, ACT UP sent a delegation to the nation's capital for the second national gay rights march on Washington. The first march had taken place in 1979; it had been mounted in response to the 1978 assassination of Harvey Milk, who had served as one of San Francisco's first openly gay elected officials. The second march took place on the afternoon of October 11, 1987. It demonstrated the growing ties within the LGBTQ community and the objections its members had to the conservative tilt of the Reagan administration, the Supreme Court's 1986 *Bowers v. Hardwick* decision, and federal neglect of the AIDS crisis.

President Reagan's silence about AIDS had barely been broken since he'd finally publicly mentioned the syndrome in 1985. He had waited until May 31, 1987, to deliver his first policy speech about AIDS and to establish a presidential commission to study it. (A year later his administration largely dismissed the nearly six hundred recommendations of the group as incompatible with its commitment to reducing domestic spending.) After the Democratic Party regained control of Congress in 1987, lawmakers were able to fund a series of measures to support HIV/AIDS research, testing, prevention, and treatment. But conservative opposition remained.

That same year North Carolina Republican senator Jesse Helms, a longtime antagonist of the gay community, proposed a successful anti-AIDS education amendment. His measure prohibited federal spending on any literature that might seem to condone homosexual sex or promote illegal drug use. It effectively hampered efforts to inform at-risk communities about life-saving prevention and harm reduction strategies for combating the spread of HIV.

In addition, in 1987 Reagan's public health office imposed a fear-based, unscientific ban of all HIV-positive people from entering the United States. The prohibition stood for twenty-two years and prompted a sustained protest by the international scientific community, which refused to hold its annual AIDS conferences on American soil until the exclusion was lifted. Such restrictions and the overriding concerns of the thousands of people who lived under the cloud of AIDS literally drove people into the streets.

"I remember chanting, *we'll never be silent again!*" Ron Goldberg recalled of the October 1987 gay rights march in Washington, DC. "And the people on the sidewalk initially thought that maybe we were yelling at them. But then they realized, no, we're the 'we.' And by the end of that weekend everybody in town was wearing SILENCE = DEATH T-shirts and buttons. I looked around and went, 'Oh my god, this is something. This is going to be a movement.'"

And he was right.

CHAPTER 9

COVERAGE

1987–1988

DURING 1987, the same year New Yorkers launched ACT UP, Cleve Jones and a bunch of his friends in San Francisco were sewing furiously. Jones had become an activist after moving to the Bay Area in the 1970s and had helped secure Harvey Milk's landmark 1978 election. Milk and the city's mayor were assassinated just eleven months later.

San Franciscans began commemorating these deaths with an annual march, and, at the 1985 event, Jones suggested that the crowd also recognize the growing number of people from the Bay Area who were dying of AIDS. He encouraged participants to write the names of lost friends or lovers on large placards, which were then connected together to form a backdrop for the outdoor service. When Jones stepped back to study the hanging cards, he immediately thought of a patchwork quilt. And that's when the lightning of creativity struck. His imagination leapt to an actual quilt—one commemorating the dead from all over the country. One that could be spread over the lawn of the National Mall in Washington, DC.

Thus was born the NAMES Project AIDS Memorial Quilt.

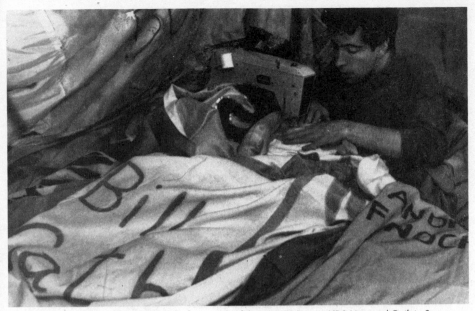

Joseph Durant pieces together some of the first panels of the NAMES Project AIDS Memorial Quilt in San Francisco, June 1987. Durant helped Cleve Jones conceptualize the quilt and was among its earliest volunteers.

By 1987 Jones had assembled a team of allies to transform his vision into action. They began by making grave-sized, three-by-six-foot panels. Word of the quilt spread. Family members, partners, and friends all around the country sewed, embroidered, printed, painted, or glued together fabric tributes to lost loved ones. Then they shipped them to Jones's new organization in San Francisco. There volunteers led by Cindy "Gert" McMullin joined panels into larger blocks that were akin to the squares of an ever-growing patchwork quilt.

Jones deliberately timed the inaugural display of the AIDS memorial quilt to coincide with the LGBTQ national march on Washington—the same one that drew ACT UP protesters and their chants of *We'll never be silent again.* On the morning of October 11, 1987, volunteers unfolded the giant quilt blocks on the National Mall. The installation contained 1,920 panels and filled an area larger than a football field. Rock Hudson had a quilt panel. Poster

Boy Bobbi Campbell's name dominated a hot-pink block created by fellow San Franciscan Gilbert Baker, the man who had designed the iconic LGBTQ rainbow flag a decade earlier. But most of the quilt's multipanel blocks contained personal tributes to ordinary people. Someone's lover from New York. A friend from Montana. An African American man from Atlanta who'd been deaf and whose panel by his white lover included the American Sign Language sign for "I love you."

The AIDS memorial quilt gave an unforgettable and personal face to the growing pandemic—an expression of loss and of love that united individual stories into a national grief. After its debut, people from across the country clamored to see it. Jones and others wrangled the quilt into a truck they named Stella, and Debra Resnik stepped forward to drive the rig and the quilt on a twenty-city tour. Jones, Resnik, and other volunteers didn't just display the quilt at their appointed stops; their visits became opportunities for education, advocacy, and local AIDS-related fund-raising. And the quilt kept growing, doubling and then tripling in size. When it returned to the nation's capital in the fall of 1988, just one year after its initial unveiling, it had gone from 1,920 individual panels to over 8,000.

While the AIDS memorial quilt was on its spring tour, ACT UP returned to Wall Street to mark the first anniversary of its founding and its original action. The March 24, 1988 protest eclipsed the previous year's in scope, scale, and ingenuity. Anticipating how police would respond to their efforts, activists prepared four waves of demonstrators to swarm the scene. Each time police thought they'd cleared protesters from the pavement, another wave arrived. The phased action snarled traffic for hours on multiple streets, led to 111 arrests, and generated significant news coverage, not just about the protest but about the group's advocacy for AIDS funding, research, and treatment, too.

By this time ACT UP chapters had begun to develop in other

parts of the country and beyond. Eventually the organization would include as many as 10,000 members in nearly 150 chapters and more than a dozen countries. In early May 1988, this growing network staged simultaneous demonstrations in more than fifty cities for nine consecutive days. They called the protest Nine Days of Rage. Each day focused on a particular challenge of the AIDS pandemic and sought to draw attention to the growing constituencies of PWAs, including people of color, women, children, and the incarcerated.

On the ninth day, organizers asked participants to protest at their state capitals, so ACT UP New York massed in Albany. They chanted. They displayed a portion of the AIDS memorial quilt. They rallied for speeches. And they danced. They danced in affirmation after a speech by film historian Vito Russo, a speech that ACT UP chant coordinator Ron Goldberg has characterized as "the greatest speech I've ever heard in my life."

Russo was a legendary figure in the quest for LGBTQ rights. Actress and friend Lily Tomlin noted, "During times when it was difficult to have faith in 'leaders' it was always easy and comforting to have faith in Vito." Russo "had an amazing capacity to take any kind of adversity and turn it into something to fuel his passion and his anger and his activism," filmmaker Jeffrey Friedman observed. He knew how to channel the intensity of his rage into a call for action, writer Jewelle Gomez recalled. "You could stay with his rant until we got to something we could do."

On May 9, 1988, Russo delivered an epic rant. He affirmed his commitment as an HIV-positive gay man who intended to survive AIDS. He blasted the mentality of a society and government that had ignored the health crisis for four years until outlets like *LIFE* magazine had observed, as he put it: "it's time to pay attention, because the disease is now beginning to strike the rest of us."

Russo listed the challenges that he and others faced in the fight against AIDS.

Vito Russo repeating the remarks from his Albany speech during a protest in Washington, DC, October 10, 1988.

Homophobia.

Racism.

Indifference.

Red tape.

Conservative lawmakers such as US senator Jesse Helms.

A disinterested president.

Sensational media outlets.

He continued. "If I'm dying from anything—I'm dying from the fact that not enough rich, white, heterosexual men have gotten AIDS for anybody to give a shit." He lamented how the syndrome remained too easy to dismiss by what he derisively referred to as "the 'real' people" of America. To this segment of society, he noted, AIDS was seen as something that only affected "the disposable populations of fags and junkies who deserve what they get." He observed that these people "don't spend their waking hours going from hospital room to hospital room, and watching the people that they love die slowly of neglect and bigotry." He added: "They haven't been to two funerals a week for the last three or four or five years—so they don't give a shit, because it's not happening to them."

Near the end of his speech, to cheering and applause, Russo said, "Someday, the AIDS crisis will be over. Remember that. And when that day comes, when that day has come and gone, there will be people alive on this earth—gay people and straight people, men and women, black and white—who will hear the story that once there was a terrible disease in this country, and all over the world, and that a brave group of people stood up and fought and, in some cases, gave their lives, so that other people might live and be free." Ever the fighter, he ended his speech with a closing salvo: "And then, after we kick the shit out of this disease, we're all going to be alive to kick the shit out of this system, so that this never happens again."

▲

What Russo didn't know at the time of his speech was that a top federal official—Surgeon General C. Everett Koop—had begun to agree with him. When Russo spoke in Albany, he complained about the lack of attention given to educating the general public about AIDS. "We are being allowed to die, while low-risk populations are being panicked—not educated, panicked—into believing that we deserve to die." Although the surgeon general, the nation's leading physician, shared Reagan's conservative principles, the mounting toll of the pandemic appalled Koop. After Reagan's reelection, Koop seized on a stray presidential comment, ignored past directions to avoid discussing the crisis, and aimed the megaphone of the surgeon general's office toward AIDS education.

His initiative resulted in the 1988 mailing to every single American household of an eight-page brochure called "Understanding AIDS." Never before or since has the federal government attempted such a broad outreach on a subject of public health. The campaign distributed more than 100 million English-language copies of the pamphlet and 4 million copies in Spanish. Translations were available in six other languages, as well as in Braille and on audiotape. The Democratically controlled Congress passed a special appropriation of funds to cover the expense of nearly $25 million.

"Understanding AIDS" followed the same strategy as the prevention literature that had sprung up within the gay community in earlier years: It didn't mince words. Americans encountered, often for the first time, frank discussions about the use of condoms, oral sex, anal sex, semen, and, as the text put it, "shooting drugs." "Some of the issues involved in this brochure may not be things you are used to discussing openly," Koop wrote in an introductory statement. "I can easily understand that. But now you must discuss them. We must all know about AIDS. Read this brochure and talk about it with those you love." He added, "I encourage you to practice responsible behavior based on understanding and strong personal values. That is what you can do to stop AIDS."

Articles in the booklet addressed in straightforward terms the sexual acts that contributed to the spread of HIV: "Anal intercourse, with or without a condom, is risky," it stated, among other observations. It reviewed the many ways one could not get AIDS. "You won't get AIDS from saliva, sweat, tears, urine, or a bowel movement." It detailed risky behaviors such as having "unprotected sex (without a condom) with an infected person." The brochure explained why parents needed to discuss the subject with their children: "Children hear about AIDS, just as we all do. But they don't understand it, so they become frightened." As part of his campaign, Koop coordinated with the CDC to establish state and national telephone hotlines, anticipating that citizens would want to know even more about AIDS prevention and care.

In its first month the nationwide number received more than a quarter of a million calls.

CHAPTER 10

FURY

1988–1989

"I'M here today because I don't want a quilt with my name on it in front of the White House next year," Vito Russo told reporters at a press conference in Washington, DC, on October 10, 1988, as activists massed in the nation's capital. He and others were gathering to view the second display of the AIDS memorial quilt, and many of them planned to participate in the most ambitious ACT UP action yet: Seize Control of the FDA. The next day Russo was one of more than a thousand protestors from around the country who massed outside the federal drug approval agency with the goal of occupying its Rockville, Maryland, headquarters. Noting that other countries were able to bring medications safely to market more rapidly than the United States, the activists attempted yet again to focus media attention on America's tediously slow drug approval process.

Many protesters wrapped themselves in red tape to symbolize the constraints of the federal bureaucracy. Others carried fake tombstones and stretched out on the pavement in clusters of living graveyards—what they called a die-in. Peter Staley from ACT

ACT UP activists mass outside the Federal Drug Administration headquarters, October 11, 1988. The Seize Control of the FDA protest drew nationwide media attention to the HIV/AIDS epidemic.

UP New York climbed onto the massive awning that overhung the building's entrance and suspended an enormous SILENCE = DEATH banner above it. Fellow New Yorker David Wojnarowicz lettered the back of his trademark ACT UP bomber jacket with the words "If I die of AIDS—forget burial—just drop my body on the steps of the FDA."

Signs reinforced the day's themes. TIME *ISN'T* THE ONLY THING THE FDA IS KILLING, read one. Another message, newly created for ACT UP by the Gran Fury arts collective, appeared on shirts and placards. Accompanied by a blood-red handprint its text said: THE GOVERNMENT HAS BLOOD ON ITS HANDS. ONE AIDS DEATH EVERY HALF HOUR. Throughout the eight-hour occupation, protesters spoke with the many reporters covering the scene, were arrested by the busload, made noise, and shouted strategic chants.

Seize control. Seize control.

Forty-two thousand dead of AIDS, where was the FDA?

Release the drugs now. Release the drugs now.

We die / they do nothing. We die / they do nothing.

Shame! Shame! Shame!

The following week, FDA officials announced plans to expedite its drug approval process even further.

That news was one of the more promising developments of 1988. By the end of the year, Ronald Reagan's vice president, George H. W. Bush, had been elected president, signaling the likely continuation of his predecessor's conservative-leaning politics and policies. In New York, members of ACT UP continued to read aloud the names of the recently deceased at their weekly meetings and to plot their next moves against the indifference of yet another administration. And every week AIDS relentlessly thinned the activists' ranks.

Back in 1981, it had seemed inconceivable that the few hundred cases known then as GRID were the leading edge of a health crisis that might rival—or even surpass—all previous human epidemics in killing power and global reach. The most recent pandemic, the Hong Kong flu of 1968, had killed as many as 4 million people. The influenza outbreak of 1918–1919, as catastrophically destructive as it had been (estimates of fatalities range widely from 25 to 50 million or more), had at least been of relatively short duration. But AIDS was different. AIDS was like an unwelcome houseguest who refused to go home. Or a war that never ended.

Ever.

Deaths from AIDS and the pace of HIV infections continued to accelerate in the United States and beyond. The availability of testing accounted for some of this increase—testing made it possible to identify more PWAs—but the rate of infections and deaths also rose because enough time had passed for symptoms of AIDS to emerge among people who had been infected unwittingly during the 1970s and early 1980s.

Although the initial concentrations of illness began among white gay men in New York and on the West Coast, African American men were affected from the beginning. Michael Gottlieb, one of the Los Angeles doctors who had noted the "unusual" occurrence of pneumonia in five gay men in 1981, saw the same symptoms in a gay black man with his sixth case.

As the eighties unfolded, the syndrome took hold in urban centers across the country, blazing through communities of color, particularly in the South. These areas already faced endemic racism and poverty. HIV introduced yet another challenge to residents who lacked access to healthcare, harm reduction programs, and other prevention efforts. Faith-based and cultural traditions that stigmatize homosexuality added further pressures on many gay people of color. But condemnation within communities didn't stop sexual behaviors or illicit drug use; it just drove risk-taking further underground and further away from potential resources.

African Americans had an additional reason to distrust public health communications and initiatives. The public had learned only the previous decade about a secret federal health examination of black men in Tuskegee, Alabama. During a long-term study of the effects of syphilis, researchers had failed to offer treatment to participants after one became available in year fifteen. Instead they had maintained their observations as a scientific experiment for another twenty-five years, allowing the men to sicken and die without appropriate care. The Tuskegee study ended only after news reporters exposed it in 1972. The researchers' rationale for denying treatment failed all ethical standards and reeked of racism. This abuse and betrayal resulted in an enduring mistrust of public health initiatives within African American communities, including those aimed at preventing the spread of HIV/AIDS.

▲

During President George H. W. Bush's first year in office, the total number of HIV-positive Americans passed the 100,000 mark for the first time. As the infected population diversified, so did the pathways for the virus's spread, a fact that increasingly put women, children, and impoverished people at risk of exposure. In the wake of the growing public health crisis, Congress had to enact a program to support HIV-infected infants whose parents abandoned them at hospitals after birth, and they established funds to provide medical care and support services for uninsured and underinsured people living with HIV/AIDS.

Federal efforts continued to fall short, though, and an increasing number of non-governmental groups and individuals took on leadership roles. The American Foundation for AIDS Research, otherwise known as amfAR, raised hundreds of millions of dollars for AIDS research, education, policy development, and treatment. Actress Elizabeth Taylor, a friend of Rock Hudson and a fellow star, devoted decades to raising funds for amfAR and supporting her own AIDS-related foundation.

Personalities as varied as Princess Diana, Yoko Ono, Judith Light, Susan Sarandon, and Elton John devoted their talents to the cause. Book publisher Scholastic stepped in to fill an education void among schoolchildren with a sustained program of articles, newsletters, and teachers' guides that provided age-appropriate material to as many as half of the nation's students. PBS collaborated with ABC on an information-based after-school drama for teens, and CBS produced its own TV special for the same audience. Films and other television programs addressed the topic, too, including NBC's 1985 TV drama *An Early Frost*, which was the first major film about AIDS. Other dramatizations followed, including biopics about Ryan White and Olympian Greg Louganis.

Meanwhile ACT UP kept pressuring government agencies and pharmaceutical companies to develop and release new and better medications. Despite the group's success in accelerating the FDA's approval process, the handful of additional HIV/AIDS drugs that made their way into medicine cabinets proved disappointing. Just being able to afford them was problematic for many. "I'm horrified at the possibility of not being able to care for myself as I and my physicians best see fit," veteran activist Marty Robinson admitted as the decade moved to a close. And, by the measure that mattered most—survival—the results from newer medications were not much different from AZT's. People got better for a while, but then they relapsed and died.

Activists also persisted in their push for better education and prevention efforts, but conservatives continued to criticize the two most effective methods for curtailing the spread of HIV: the use of condoms and the establishment of needle exchanges for intravenous drug users. Harm reduction programs that exchanged dirty needles for clean ones and prevention campaigns that distributed free condoms were just "dragging down the standards of all society," said Cardinal John O'Connor, the archbishop of New York's Catholic Church. Social conservatives were, in effect, placing their definitions of morality ahead of practical steps that could save human lives.

Women's health advocates were already angry with O'Connor for his disregard of women's reproductive rights, so in 1989 they joined with ACT UP to mount a major protest against the cardinal and the Catholic Church. After months of deliberation and planning, the group held its action on December 10. They named it Stop the Church. The effort involved some 4,500 demonstrators, most of them outside St. Patrick's Cathedral on Fifth Avenue in Manhattan where they protested in bitterly cold weather. Many wore the ACT UP uniform of combat boots, jeans, and leather jackets. Others came costumed as clowns and religious figures. Collectively they blocked traffic, chanted, blew air horns, and waved placards.

Many of the signs bore a particularly blunt message for O'Connor. It featured a provocative image of the cardinal in full vestments next

Aerial view of the AIDS Memorial Quilt during its second display in the nation's capital, October 8, 1988. The White House is visible beyond the quilt on the adjoining Ellipse.

to a fully extended condom. The pointed peak of the cardinal's miter cap aligned with the pointed tip of the condom. KNOW YOUR SCUMBAGS, advised the oversized red lettering that accompanied the illustrations. Tiny text under the condom added: THIS ONE PREVENTS AIDS.

Other placards proclaimed equally confrontational messages:

CURB YOUR DOGMA.

PAPAL BULL.

CONDOMS NOT COFFINS.

Designated protesters staged die-ins en masse in the middle of Fifth Avenue. When police officers began carrying them away for arrest on stretchers, other volunteers took their places. The pre-arranged choreography of protest transformed the major thorough-fare into an aboveground cemetery, complete with fake tombstones. DIVA TV filmed the proceedings while nearby activists chanted re-minders of *no violence, no violence* at arresting police officers.

Meanwhile a number of affinity groups had infiltrated the church sanctuary in preparation for implementing a series of independent actions during the cardinal's homily, or sermon. Two men handcuffed themselves to a church pew. Thirty people gathered in the center aisle to stage a noisy die-in, complete with the blowing of whistles and a confetti-style shower of condoms. A different group scattered themselves throughout the congregation and took turns standing and calling out rehearsed statements to O'Connor.

Michael Petrelis, the veteran Lavender Hill Mob protester, became caught up in the moment, veered off script, climbed onto a church pew, and repeatedly screamed, "O'Connor, you're killing us! You're killing us, just stop it! Stop it!" Police arrested him and used stretchers to haul die-in protesters out of the sanctuary.

Members and friends of an affinity group known as the Hail Marys lined up with other parishioners during Communion. Instead of repeating the standard ritual text, each activist delivered a statement of protest. "Safe sex is moral sex!" said one person. "I support a woman's right to choose!" replied another. "Condoms save lives!" someone else said. Sean Strub has described in *Body Counts* how he found himself compelled on the spot to honor Michael, his deceased partner: "May the Lord bless the man I love, who died a year ago this week." When a priest handed protester Tom Keane a Communion wafer with the customary words that honored it as the body of Christ, Keane replied, "Opposing safe-sex education is murder."

Then he crumbled the wafer in his hand and, in defiance of the church, dropped its sacred fragments onto the floor.

CHAPTER 11

OUTLOOK

1990–1992

BY the early 1990s, the outlook in America could not have seemed grimmer for PWAs. A decade had elapsed since the emergence of AIDS. But, despite the research, despite the development of drugs, despite the heroics of physicians and community groups, despite the activism, people kept dying. Nothing stopped it. Even though additional medications continued to reach the marketplace, none of them proved effective at keeping HIV in check.

President George H. W. Bush had followed his predecessor's example and focused on different domestic and international priorities, not AIDS. He waited more than a year to deliver a public speech on the subject. By 1992, three years into his administration, the number of HIV-positive Americans had tripled to 300,000. Well over 100,000 PWAs had died, and AIDS had become the leading cause of death in the United States for men aged twenty-five to forty-four.

ACT UP's Stop the Church action, which took place during Bush's first year in office, had been a huge success by past measures. Police had arrested more than one hundred demonstrators,

Larry Kramer (right) consoles Vito Russo, July 1, 1990. Russo died four months later at the age of forty-four.

and the press had covered the protest extensively. But the shock value of certain elements—particularly Tom Keane's off-script desecration of a Communion wafer and Michael Petrelis's impromptu screaming at Cardinal O'Connor—divided responses to the action and generated enormous criticism of the protest as an attack on religion. Even beforehand some ACT UP members had raised concerns about interrupting a sacred ceremony. The bickering showed how challenging it was to sustain consensus and momentum during a long-term crisis.

And so the fight against HIV/AIDS continued, mimicking the virus itself. The ill, the infected, their allies, and their organizations adapted and evolved, whether fighting the enemy within or the forces of resistance outside: discrimination, neglect, and inertia. Some injustices were corrected more quickly than others. The Americans with Disabilities Act of 1990 made it illegal to discriminate against people who exhibited the end-stage symptoms of AIDS; later, after HIV/AIDS became the official name of the syndrome in 1998, the legislation began covering not just those who were dying because of AIDS but anyone who was HIV-positive. Even so the infected or ill were at risk of being excluded from access to health insurance if they applied for coverage with HIV/AIDS as a preexisting condition. And it would be another twelve years before the passage of the Affordable Care Act required insurance carriers to provide coverage regardless of ongoing illness.

It took even longer for same-sex partners to gain equal rights; throughout the AIDS pandemic lifelong partners remained at risk of being excluded from deathbeds, omitted from lists of loved ones in obituaries, and contested in matters of financial inheritance because they lacked the legal standing of marriage. Members of the LGBTQ community only gained the nationwide guarantee of those rights with the Supreme Court's 2015 landmark marriage equality ruling, *Obergefell v. Hodges*.

▲

One bright spot during 1990 within ACT UP was the progress being made by an affinity group known as the Treatment + Data Committee, or T+D. This group had formed early in the organization's history after a middle-aged, heterosexual scientist named Iris Long began attending meetings. Long, who admitted she had not knowingly met a gay person until she volunteered at GMHC and then ACT UP, offered to share her expertise as a pharmaceutical chemist with other members. In the months that followed, an unlikely combination of intelligent but distinctly unscientific allies joined her in a sort of study group.

Playwright and author Jim Eigo proved adept at decoding Long's technical statements into something others were more nearly able to understand. Punk rocker Mark Harrington compiled a forty-eight-page glossary of medical jargon to help himself make sense of all the terminology; his dictionary proved to be so invaluable that organizers duplicated it for wider use. Architect David Z. Kirschenbaum collaborated with attorney David Barr to pry health policy data out of federal agencies. Peter Staley contributed the financial savvy he'd gained during his years of experience on Wall Street as a bond trader. Other T+D members included teenager Garance Franke-Ruta and college dropouts Spencer Cox and Derek Link.

One of the group's first major successes was the brainchild of Eigo: a drug testing process he called the parallel track system. His proposal called for adding an extra set of participants to various drug trials. The original study could proceed according to prescribed scientific standards; meanwhile the second, less strictly controlled group of subjects could access medications in a parallel study that could yield additional useful data. His idea addressed two problems. First, it got drugs to market faster by increasing the wealth of research. Second, it expanded the pool of people who could access medications. Making experimental drugs available to additional people gave them the chance to live longer. Without it, they would have died anyway. With it, maybe they'd live after all.

Members of T+D began contacting officials at the National Institutes of Health, or NIH, trying to convince its scientists to integrate the parallel track system into the government's drug testing procedures. It was slow work, in part because each group eyed the other warily. Over time activists and researchers established a sometimes testy, sometimes collaborative, but generally workable relationship. Much of the communication flowed through Anthony Fauci, the head of the National Institute of Allergy and Infectious Diseases at NIH and the institute's point person on AIDS. It took two years of trust-building, diplomacy, and persuasion, but Fauci and others finally endorsed Eigo's basic framework and adopted the parallel track method of drug testing for AIDS medications.

That decision came on the eve of ACT UP's next major action, one that targeted Fauci and federal researchers at the heart of his domain, the sprawling NIH campus in Bethesda, Maryland. Even with T+D's progress, organizers wanted to keep up pressure on Fauci, his institute, and the federal government in general. Research dollars continued to lag, and so did progress on finding a way to outwit HIV. Storm the NIH, organizers dubbed the effort, and they set the action for May 21, 1990.

The night before, protesters gathered for a meeting that was part review, part pep-rally. Between moments of business, activist Tony Malliaris fired up the crowd by performing a rap that he'd composed for the occasion. His creative lyrics managed to rhyme complicated

Police officers arrest a demonstrator during protests at the CDC, December 3, 1990. They detained one hundred people who were advocating for increased attention to the needs of HIV-positive women.

medical terms, present piercing summaries of pandemic history, and pull the audience into an irresistible refrain of *Storm the NIH*. His performance ended with a final challenge:

> So if the quality fades, a commissioner jades,
>   or somebody grades a person with AIDS,
> They better change their ways, or we're on a bus—
>   you ever been embarrassed by a thousand of us?
> We're ACT UP!
> We demand healthcare for all, summer to spring,
>   winter to fall.
> We don't act without cause, but before too long,
>   if ACT UP's there, then something's wrong.
> Yeah, right?
> This is a trial by jury of straights and queers.
>   We're saying save lives, and not careers.
> We're fired up for tomorrow morn.
> Remember, if you don't like something, change it!

At which point the closing call-and-response chorus kicked in as Malliaris answered repetitive audience cries of *Storm the NIH* with his own successive beats for action.

Let's go.
This is war.
For the sick.
For the poor.
Act up!
Fight back!
Fight AIDS!

And the next morning, they did.

A thousand protesters swarmed the sprawling NIH campus. Affinity groups with names such as Chain Gang, Awning Leapers,

InVisible Women, and Dos Locos Radicales made their way toward a stately brick building at the heart of the property where Fauci maintained an office. FAUCI, YOU'RE KILLING US, one of the day's signs read in a reference to the deaths that continued to mount because of lagging research funding. Protesters massed on the pavement and lawns outside the impressive portico and put their plans into action. Designated protesters ignited flares atop towering poles, setting adrift individual streams of rainbow-colored smoke until they melded

ACT UP recruitment poster for its Storm the NIH protest, 1990. The poster played off a well-known advertising campaign for Coca-Cola and included fine print condemning the lack of drug development and accusing Burroughs Wellcome of capitalizing on its monopoly.

into a darkening cloud. Signs, chants, and speeches called for the NIH to pay more attention to the impact AIDS was having on women and people of color. Activists demanded that the nation's leading medical research center work harder and faster to develop better medications. Journalists and camera crews captured the protests in reports that would reach a national audience on that evening's news.

The prominent coverage pleased Bob Rafsky, a former public relations executive who served as ACT UP's media coordinator. "The country as a whole saw something very powerful on TV that night on all three networks." But the activists knew that change required constant pressure. A few weeks later Rafsky noted: "For all the work that we've done, we haven't yet done the work, and for all the secrets we've unlocked, we haven't yet found the secret of stopping this epidemic." He added, "We have a lot of work to do."

Actions large and small followed, including one that T+D member Peter Staley organized with a few study group participants and other allies, including Sean Strub. Together they targeted the conservative US senator gays loved to hate: Republican Jesse Helms. On September 5, 1991, to protest Helms's longstanding rejection of promoting condom usage, the group enveloped his suburban Virginia home in a thirty-five-foot-tall, fully inflated prophylactic emblazoned with the statement A CONDOM TO STOP UNSAFE POLITICS. HELMS IS DEADLIER THAN A VIRUS. Staley judged the action a success. He observed that Helms, who was not home at the time, "never again proposed or passed a life-threatening AIDS amendment."

▲

As the fight against AIDS entered its second decade, tensions grew within ACT UP, and its old consensus-built model of governance frayed. On one occasion Larry Kramer became so frustrated listening to activists bicker that he interrupted the squabble to shout. "Plague! We are in the middle of a plague!" he yelled. "And you behave like this!" Kramer, having coupled the F-word with plague for added emphasis in his opening sentence, used it again in the one that followed. "Plague! Forty million infected people is a plague! We are in the worst shape we have ever, ever, ever been in. All those pills we're shoveling down our throats? Forget it," he shouted. Later, as his voice began to calm, he observed, "I say to you in year ten the same thing I said to you in 1981 when there were forty-one cases: Until we get our acts together, all of us, we are as good as dead."

Before the year was out, ongoing arguments about strategies and tactics prompted key members of T+D to leave ACT UP entirely. Core participants had drawn increasing criticism for their deepening ties to Fauci at the NIH, other federal researchers, and scientists who worked for the pharmaceutical industry. Such outreach seemed like a betrayal of the revolutionary principles of ACT UP, as if the committee had become allied with the enemy.

The leaders of T+D disagreed. They viewed the evolving teamwork as an essential step in the quest for progress. In late 1991 a core group of them—including Peter Staley, Mark Harrington, Garance Franke-Ruta, and Spencer Cox—left ACT UP to form what became known as TAG, short for Treatment Action Group. In time TAG would outshine its ACT UP parent, but both organizations persevered in the fight.

During the 1992 presidential election year, Bill Clinton was among the Democrats who vied for the chance to unseat George H. W. Bush. ACT UP activist Bob Rafsky confronted the young candidate that spring at a New York campaign event. "We're *dying*," he'd shouted. "What are you going to do about AIDS?" Clinton criticized Rafsky's heckling style, then offered what became a famous response: "I feel your pain." He went on to say, "If you want somebody that'll fight AIDS, vote for me, because when I come in to do something, I do it, and I fight for it."

Such comments helped earn Clinton the support of the LGBTQ community, but Rafsky knew whatever help Clinton offered wouldn't come in time to save him. A few weeks after his verbal tussle with Clinton, Rafsky wrote in the *New York Times*, "I'll try to die a good death, if I can figure out what one is."

Later that year Rafsky was among those who traveled to Washington, DC, as part of an ACT UP contingent that viewed the fourth display in the capital of the AIDS memorial quilt. By then the commemorative work represented people from every state and twenty-eight foreign countries and had been nominated for a Nobel Peace Prize. The 1992 display filled much of the 146-acre National Mall, the equivalent of more than one hundred football fields. Among its thousands of panels was a new one that read: "My name is Duane Kearns Puryear. I was born on December 20, 1964. I was diagnosed with AIDS on September 7, 1987 at 4:45 PM. I was 22 years old. Sometimes, it makes me very sad. I made this panel myself. If you are reading it, I am dead . . ."

The next day, October 11, ACT UP members mounted what they called the Ashes Action. Republican presidents had "turned people we love into ashes and bone chips and corpses," declared David Robinson, as hundreds prepared to march to the White House, some with blood-red paint on their palms, faces, or clothing. "We are not going to hide this anymore," he added. To the cadence of a solemn drum roll, the marchers chanted such statements as:

History will recall, Reagan and Bush did nothing at all.
George Bush, you can't hide. We charge you with genocide.
Bringing the dead to your door. We won't take it anymore.

As the protesters approached the perimeter of the White House grounds, riot police, some on horseback, tried to push them back, but a cluster of people surged forward. Amidst a cacophony of screaming and crying within the crowd, they launched the ashes of their loved ones over the spiked iron fence and watched them settle onto the president's lawn. This intensely emotional act reflected the increasing anger and desperation of protesters—including the deceased, some of whom had made dying wishes for their remains to become weapons in the continuing fight.

Bob Rafsky addressed members of ACT UP back in New York after the protest. He joked about the pre-event jitters of the coordinator, who was leading his first action, then noted, "When I saw him pressed against the White House fence by all our bodies, kneeling and weeping, as ashes soared over him, I felt for certain that he would never have that nightmare again."

Then Rafsky spoke about how the protest had been, as he called it, cathartic on a number of levels. It was a way to grieve those now resting on the White House lawn. It was a way to grieve the countless others who had died because of AIDS. And it was a way to acknowledge a changing of the guard within ACT UP.

Time was running out, he said, for people like himself and ACT UP founding member David Robinson, who had spoken at the protest. "In a certain sense, it was our funeral, too, in that we were not so much needing it, as passing through it, and handing the baton of leadership, or what you will, to a new generation of AIDS activists who, with this action, wholly and completely emerge, so that the ashes which we mourn are also the ashes from which we rise."

Rafsky added: "My most fervent hope for this new generation of activists is that, before you have to take on the burden of inspiring yet another generation of activists, your work will be done."

PART THREE
CONTROL
1992–Today

Activists carry the coffin of Mark Lowe Fisher in protest through the streets of New York City, November 2, 1992.

"Let the whole earth hear us now: We beg, we pray, we demand that this epidemic end, not just so we may live, but so that Mark's soul may rest in peace at last." —Bob Rafsky, 1992

CHAPTER 12

LOST

1992–1996

HIV began spreading more rapidly within communities of color during the late 1980s and early 1990s when America's urban centers were hit by an increased use of heroin and the arrival of the street drug crack. Many of these neighborhoods were already burdened by poverty and lacked the advocates and resources to handle the added social disruptions of addiction. Ongoing federal opposition to needle exchanges fueled the spread of HIV between drug users, and from there the virus traveled via sexual intercourse to partners male and female. Infected women faced the added risk of exposing unborn and nursing children to the virus. When HIV infections accelerated along with the drug use epidemic, some community leaders set aside their former objections and began distributing condoms and clean needles. But the widening web of infection was hard to contain.

Basketball legend Earvin "Magic" Johnson helped to champion community intervention efforts after his 1991 disclosure that he had contracted HIV through unprotected sex. This discovery disrupted his NBA career but not his role on the public stage. Johnson pivoted almost immediately from basketball to health activism and initiated an ongoing effort to reduce AIDS-related stigma. He encouraged young people to practice safe sex and to be tested if they were at risk of infection.

Johnson showed by example that a heterosexual black man could not just survive with AIDS—he could thrive. Even though he stopped playing with the Los Angeles Lakers, he joined other US athletes on the 1992 gold-medal-winning Olympic men's basketball team—otherwise known as the Dream Team. He used his voice and fame in additional ways, too, slamming then president George H. W. Bush for his lack of healthcare leadership. "I cannot in good conscience continue to serve on a commission whose important work is so utterly ignored by your administration," he stated that fall when he withdrew from Bush's National Commission on AIDS.

Bush lost his reelection bid six weeks after Johnson's resignation,

Local volunteers distribute informational material about HIV/AIDS to residents in Atlanta, Georgia, August 22, 1987.

and Bill Clinton was sworn in as the new president on January 20, 1993. The next month Bob Rafsky, the man who had challenged Clinton to do something about AIDS during the campaign, died at age forty-seven. Among his grieving survivors was a seven-year-old daughter, Sara.

Hopes about Clinton's administration faded rapidly within the LGBTQ community when he failed to deliver on his campaign promises, such as one to implement the recommendations from past presidential commissions on AIDS, and so the activism continued. TAG pressed onward with the medical establishment, and ACT UP staged more protests.

One action grew out of the deathbed request of thirty-five-year-old activist and former menswear designer Tim Bailey. Initially he had asked friends to throw his body over the gates of the White House; later he agreed to an outdoor funeral there instead. Organizers planned what they called a political funeral and traveled with his corpse to Washington, DC, in July 1993 to stage the action. When the capital police realized a protest was beginning to form, they called in human and canine reinforcements to stop the demonstration. At one point officers tried to wrest Bailey's open coffin from the hands of ACT UP members. "What the hell are you afraid of?" David Robinson yelled at the authorities. "That ordinary citizens will see what our government is doing? Is that what you're afraid of?"

Political funerals continued throughout Clinton's first term of office. During the president's reelection bid in 1996, activists expressed their dissatisfaction with his work on AIDS by repeating their 1992 anti-Bush Ashes Action protest. Once again family members, friends, and partners tossed the cremated remains of their loved ones over the perimeter fence and onto the grounds of the White House. Included were the ashes of David Wojnarowicz, who had taken part in the Seize Control of the FDA action eight years earlier and lettered his ACT UP jacket with a demand to have his body deposited on the steps of the FDA. The 1996 scattering of his ashes was a near-literal realization of his request. The White House lawn is the unmarked final resting place for the remains of at least eighteen people who died because of HIV.

By the election year of 1996 AIDS had become the leading cause of death for all Americans—male and female—between the ages of twenty-five and forty-four. Reported cases of infection in the United States topped half a million that year, with rates still soaring in urban communities and among people of color. Before 1996 more whites were HIV-positive than blacks; starting that year black infection rates outpaced white rates despite representing a much smaller fraction of the total population. Before the end of the decade black Americans would be ten times as likely to die of AIDS as whites and three times as likely as Hispanics.

During October 1996 the AIDS memorial quilt returned to the nation's capital for what would be the last showing in its entirety. The effort required 12,000 volunteers, and its panels filled the entire length of the National Mall, from the foot of the Capitol building to the reflecting pool by the Lincoln Memorial, a distance of more than a mile. By then the quilt chronicled the passing of thousands of the 350,000 Americans who had died because of HIV/AIDS.

▲

That staggering number—350,000—is so much more than just a statistic. Individual people died to become a part of it. A lover, a son, a friend. A brother or father. A favorite teacher. A patient who had depended on someone else's blood for survival. A coworker who hid that he was gay. Or ill. Or going to die.

Consider this: HIV descimated an entire generation of actors,

Tom Fox breaks down as he adds the one hundredth name to his list of dead friends, February 15, 1989. Fox's employer, the Atlanta Journal-Constitution, documented his experiences as an HIV-positive man, including his death from AIDS on July 11, 1989, at age thirty-three.

dancers, filmmakers, and directors. Choreographer Michael Bennett of *A Chorus Line* fame, dead in 1987 at age forty-four. Choreographer Alvin Ailey, founder of the renowned African American dance troupe, lost in 1989 at age fifty-eight. Ventriloquist Wayland Flowers, in 1988 at age forty-eight. Actor Charles Ludlam, in 1987 at age forty-four. Colin Higgins, screenwriter for the cult classic *Harold and Maude* and both writer and director of the 1980 hit film *Nine to Five*, dead in 1988 at age forty-seven. Ballet genius Rudolf Nureyev, lost in 1993 at age fifty-four.

HIV ravaged the ranks of the nation's artists and musicians. Liberace, the flamboyant pianist, in 1987 at age sixty-seven. The photographer Robert Mapplethorpe, in 1989 at age forty-two. Graffiti-inspired artist Keith Haring, in 1990 at age thirty-one. Freddie Mercury of the band Queen, in 1991 at age forty-five. The rapper Eazy-E, in 1995 at age thirty-one.

HIV emptied the runways and design studios of the fashion industry. Supermodel Joe Macdonald, lost in 1983 at age thirty-seven. Perry Ellis, in 1986 at age forty-six. Willi Smith, in 1987 at age thirty-nine. Halston, in 1990 at age fifty-seven. Gone, too, were countless unsung makeup artists and stylists.

The virus silenced the voices of authors, poets, journalists, and commentators. Children's book authors and illustrators Arnold Lobel, who wrote the Frog and Toad books, lost in 1987 at age fifty-four, and John Steptoe, whose works included *Stevie*, lost in 1989 at age thirty-eight. Max Robinson, who broke ground as the nation's first African American network news anchor and founded the National Association of Black Journalists, lost in 1988 at age forty-nine. Science fiction author and commentator Isaac Asimov, lost in 1992 at age seventy-two. Arthur Ashe, a sports analyst who was also the nation's first African American tennis pro and holder of thirty-three championship titles, lost in 1993 at age forty-nine. Journalist Randy Shilts, who wrote *And the Band Played On*, the earliest history of AIDS, lost in 1994 at age forty-two.

HIV claimed the life of Bruce Mailman, the owner of the Saint, the disco so legendary its name had been informally linked to the outbreak by the phrase *Saint's disease*. It killed ten out of the eleven men who authored the Denver Principles in 1983, including safe-sex advocate Michael Callen, who died in 1993 at age thirty-eight. It killed Vito Russo, who died in 1990 at age forty-four, two years after his passionate appeal during the 1988 Days of Rage. HIV caused the deaths of Marty Robinson, age forty-nine, founder of the Lavender Hill Mob, in 1992, and Tony Malliaris, age thirty-three, the activist who rapped on the eve of Storm the NIH, in 1995.

The Ray family in Florida lost two of its three sons because of HIV. As young hemophiliacs the three brothers had become infected through transfusions during the same period as Ryan White. Like White, the Rays had faced school discrimination and community harassment. In August of 1987, shortly after a federal judge ordered them readmitted to their local classrooms, someone burned down the Rays' home. The family relocated to a more welcoming district, just as White had done. Two of the brothers later died because of their infection, Ricky in 1992 at age fifteen and Robert at age twenty-two in 2000. Randy, the youngest of the three HIV-positive brothers, has survived. Ryan White, their hemophiliac HIV-positive peer, died in 1990 at age eighteen.

Contaminated blood killed Elizabeth Glaser, too. She'd received it in 1981 when she'd needed a transfusion during the birth of her first child. The donated blood introduced HIV into her body, and she unwittingly passed the virus to her daughter through breastfeeding. Unaware of her infection, she also inadvertently infected her son during her second pregnancy. Only after her daughter developed AIDS did Glaser and her husband realize what had happened. Glaser testified before Congress and, having lost her daughter, spoke at Bill Clinton's 1992 nominating convention. She died two years later, but her son survived.

So many deaths, a tally surpassing 350,000 after 1996. And every number represents a life.

▲

New York Times reporter Jeffrey Schmalz had not only lived with AIDS, he'd covered news of the pandemic for his paper. He died in 1993 at age thirty-nine, three weeks before the publication of his parting commentary. "A miracle is possible, of course," he wrote. "And for a long time, I thought one would happen. But let's face it, a miracle isn't going to happen. One day soon I will simply become one of the 90 people in America to die that day of AIDS. It's like knowing I will be killed by a speeding car, but not knowing when or where."

"Obviously you already know the 'big story' about me," Michael Riesenberg wrote to a friend in 1993. He explained that he'd had to leave his beloved job at a New York business because "taking care of myself and keeping track of everything seems to be a job all by itself." He was encouraged by his intensive healthcare regimen. "My doctors and I have been aggressively approaching the virus; I take about fifty pills a day, and have doctor's appointments nearly every day. So far, so good." Six months later, he died at age thirty-four.

Filmmaker Peter Adair died from AIDS in 1996 when he was fifty-three. One of the people he interviewed for *Absolutely Positive* was Marlon Riggs, a fellow filmmaker, who died because of HIV in 1994 at age thirty-seven. Riggs's identity as a gay black man informed one of his early films, *Tongues Untied*, a frank documentary about the intersection of homophobia and racism. Riggs learned of his infection in 1989 while making the film.

During the *Absolutely Positive* interview, Adair asked Riggs how he coped with the burden of being HIV-positive. Riggs paused. Then he told Adair that he drew strength from the story of Harriet Tubman. "Whenever I feel low," Riggs said, "I think of this woman . . . pushing herself to find freedom, and finding it, and going back into slavery time after time to take others back to freedom with her. And I think of the tremendous risks and the tremendous courage that was required to do that, and that's enough . . . for me. . . . That's the past I draw upon that helps me through this and will help me if, when, should I get sicker and will continue to push me on, to keep saying to me:

"'One more step. We'll make it. Don't worry, child. One more step.'"

CHAPTER 13

DRUGS

1996–1997

TEN years into the crisis, theater audiences had assessed AIDS through the two-part masterpiece by playwright Tony Kushner, *Angels in America*. "This disease will be the end of many of us, but not nearly all," said central character Prior Walter at the end of the mammoth saga about the pandemic. "And the dead will be commemorated and will struggle on with the living, and we are not going away. We won't die secret deaths anymore. The world only spins forward. We will be citizens. The time has come."

By 1996 the time had come—the time to stop dying.

It had been an interminably long wait—fifteen years. During that span New York City alone had lost 100,000 people because of HIV/AIDS. So many had fought it. The sick and the well, activists and allies—together they had confronted not only HIV but innumerable other challenges.

Conservative politics.

Homophobia.

Funding shortfalls.

Research squabbles.

Red tape.

Corporate greed.

Confusion.

Desperation.

And death.

Always death.

In the end, it all came down to the science. While the federal government had provided no supplemental funding at the beginning of the crisis and insufficient appropriations for at least the next six years, by 1996 it had invested billions of dollars into HIV/AIDS research. Financial support had begun to increase in 1987, the first year of the outbreak that Democrats controlled both chambers of Congress. Allocations continued to grow during the next eight years while the party retained control over government spending.

Even after Republicans retook the House and Senate in 1995, midway through Bill Clinton's first term of office, the annual investment in research continued to increase. By then, though, the epidemic had become so destructive that the government faced an enormous annual expense just caring for those who were HIV-positive. Many people qualified for mandatory federal assistance through Medicaid, Medicare, and Social Security disability income programs. They and others also depended on government aid for medication, housing, prevention programs, and research. Over time the costs of caring for HIV-positive people

An ACT UP educational poster targets President Bill Clinton, circa 1994. The reverse side carried the same message in Spanish.

would swell, dwarfing the amount spent on prevention and scientific research.

Clues about how to outwit HIV had been emerging since the virus's discovery in 1983. It soon became clear that HIV worked in a uniquely destructive way. It didn't just invade the body, vigorously reproduce, and attempt to overwhelm the human immune system. It actually turned off that immune system by eliminating a key defensive component known then as the T cell and now by the newer scientific term, CD4 cells. Even in the early days of the epidemic, physicians had noted that their patients lacked a healthy number of these cells. The discovery that HIV destroyed them explained why AIDS—unlike every other known disease at that time—was always fatal. The human body didn't stand a chance against it. This discovery didn't immediately provide an answer on how to remedy the effects of HIV, but it did suggest two possible paths for further research: figure out how to destroy the virus or determine how to disable it. It was that work—figuring out how to combat HIV—that had taken years.

Because viruses are nimble at mutating, they are virtually impossible to eliminate, so instead of trying to destroy HIV, scientists focused instead on discovering how to hinder its action. To that end, they studied the virus until they could map its infinitesimally small components, gene by gene. Then they examined the interaction of this genetic material until they were able to identify points in its viral life cycle that were vulnerable to manipulation. They found that three enzymes regulate the ability of HIV to reproduce, and their names would become as familiar as birthdates to anyone touched by AIDS.

Reverse transcriptase.

Protease.

Integrase.

These were the keys to preventing HIV infection from advancing to the end-stage illness of AIDS. If researchers could determine how to disrupt the actions of one or more of those enzymes, they'd be able to disarm HIV. The search for effective medications led to the release in 1987 of AZT. This drug acted on the first enzyme, reverse transcriptase, by interrupting the virus's reproduction process. So did three additional drugs that came on the market in the early 1990s, but all of these medications, including AZT, only interrupted the action of the enzyme temporarily. When the virus evolved, the drugs no longer made any difference. That mechanism accounted for why AZT had delayed death, but not prevented it, when patients began taking it in the late 1980s.

It took a decade, from 1986 to 1996, for drug companies to develop, test, and begin selling medications that inhibited the second of HIV's three enzymes, protease. This enzyme controls the actions of the virus as it matures and spreads. Many people gained early access to protease inhibitors in 1995 thanks to the work of TAG member Spencer Cox. Cox devised a drug trial that allowed researchers to treat a subset of individuals with two kinds of enzyme inhibitors at the same time, something scientists had not previously been able to do. Cox's research model turned out to be brilliant. The testing proved that the virus found it difficult to mutate when drugs inhibited two of the three HIV enzymes simultaneously. Furthermore, the two-pronged treatment hampered HIV's ability to attack and destroy CD4 cells, thus preserving the patient's immune system.

Cox's approach generated such decisive results that regulators approved sale of the new protease inhibitors far more rapidly than would otherwise have happened. Activists credit him with saving thousands of lives by expanding access to these drugs during their testing phase and by moving them faster to market. After protease inhibitors went on sale in late 1995 and early 1996, doctors were able to prescribe them in concert with drugs that blocked reverse

Mark Harrington wraps his arms around Jay Funk, Saugerties, New York, July 24, 1993. Funk died the next year from HIV/AIDS at age thirty-five.

transcriptase (including less toxic doses of AZT). Initial therapies combined three or more medications in ways that disrupted the workings of reverse transcriptase and protease simultaneously. The new treatment regimen was called highly active antiretroviral therapy, or HAART.

HAART changed everything.

Some refer to this program as combination therapy because of the way it combines multiple medications into one treatment plan. Others refer to it as the drug cocktail. Eventually the medical community shortened its name to antiretroviral therapy, or ART.

It took another ten years for researchers to develop medications that disrupted the third HIV enzyme, integrase. This enzyme helps to integrate the genetic material from HIV into a host cell. Integrase inhibitors interrupt that process; the first such drug reached the market in 2007.

ART's impact was unmistakable. In 1995, more than 51,000 people had died of HIV/AIDS in the United States. That number was cut in half by 1997—to 21,846—thanks to the arrival of ART. The new regimen didn't work for everyone; some people still died while on it, depending on how advanced their infection had become and the extent to which their virus had mutated because of prior treatments. But ART did save tens of thousands of individuals whose infections had reached the end stage of AIDS, not to mention hundreds of thousands of HIV-positive people who had not yet become seriously ill.

At about the same time as the development of ART, scientists found a way to measure the presence of HIV in an individual, something known as a person's viral load. Previously doctors had relied on CD4 counts to determine the success of a treatment. If numbers increased, a person's immune system was stronger; if they plummeted, risk of succumbing to opportunistic infections rose. The new viral load tests used a different metric. Instead of assessing the status of a patient's immune system, it allowed physicians to determine the health of the virus itself. If someone's viral load went down or remained steady, then medications were holding HIV at bay. If the load went up, then that person's treatment regimen needed fine-tuning.

Symptomatic or not, anyone carrying the virus was encouraged to begin ART as a way to keep HIV in check. The results were almost unbelievable, but viral load tests confirmed the treatment plan's success. "It wasn't until we started putting the drugs in our bodies," TAG member Peter Staley recalled in the documentary *How to Survive a Plague*, that "sure enough, it happened in us, within thirty days, all of us. Undetectable. Undetectable. Undetectable."

Fellow TAG activist Mark Harrington observed in the same film: "That breakthrough we thought was going to happen in '88 or '89, if we just worked fast enough, you know it did happen. But not until '96." Pausing, he said, "And so a lot of people died"—including his close friend and former lover, Jay Funk. Then in a halting voice Harrington added, "Maybe if Reagan had started putting money into AIDS a little earlier, they wouldn't all be dead."

ART's results were so stunning that its impact earned a special name: the Lazarus effect. Doctors across the country watched patient after patient make miraculous recoveries. It was as if people were being brought back from the dead, the way the Bible reported the rising of Lazarus from his grave.

ART and its Lazarus effect offered a reprieve for millions of HIV-positive people including:

Quilt creator Cleve Jones.

Tireless critic Larry Kramer.

Olympic diver Greg Louganis.

The lone founding survivor of People with AIDS, Richard Berkowitz.

Basketball great Magic Johnson.

Absolutely Positive veterans Gregg Cassin and Jonnie Norway.

POZ magazine founder Sean Strub.

ART made the hopes of Bob Rafsky come true, even if it didn't arrive in time to save him. It stopped HIV from automatically cutting short every life it touched. It allowed the San Francisco *Bay Area Reporter* to publish an editorial on August 13, 1998, entitled "Death takes a holiday." The newspaper featured a front-page story with a headline that reduced many who read it to tears. The article explained that since 1981 every issue of the weekly paper had reported the death of someone from AIDS in its obituaries. The grimmest week had required thirty-one notices. After seventeen years, that streak had been broken. An enormous red banner headline proclaimed:

"No obits."

CHAPTER 14

REVIVAL

1997–2004

IT can be hard to rise from the dead.

The miracle of combination therapy helped people stop dying from AIDS, but it didn't offer a road map for how to start living again. Learning how to live without the threat of imminent death came with a completely different set of challenges and struggles. Just as with veterans who return from war, there were adjustments to make after enduring a protracted life-and-death struggle. No one regretted the arrival of protease inhibitors and ART. But the prospect of long-term health literally forced survivors to consider an unexpected question: *Now what?*

Many people had prepared so thoroughly for death that they had liquidated their assets. That house? The life insurance policy? Money in a retirement account? All of them could be gone. People had often sold everything in an effort to pay for the monumental costs of their illnesses. It was as if they'd settled their estates from the living side of the grave. They had done so confidently because everyone who was HIV-positive died sooner or later. So they had planned for it.

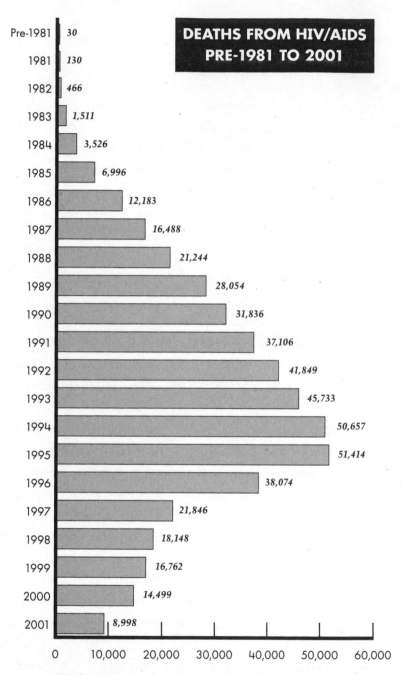

DEATHS FROM HIV/AIDS PRE-1981 TO 2001

Pre-1981	30
1981	130
1982	466
1983	1,511
1984	3,526
1985	6,996
1986	12,183
1987	16,488
1988	21,244
1989	28,054
1990	31,836
1991	37,106
1992	41,849
1993	45,733
1994	50,657
1995	51,414
1996	38,074
1997	21,846
1998	18,148
1999	16,762
2000	14,499
2001	8,998

CDC data analysis conducted by Dennis Osmond, University of California at San Francisco. An additional 360 undated deaths brings the total for this period to 467,910.

And then they stopped dying.

Survivors also had to reimagine relationships. So did friends, family members, and lovers, some of whom had been on deathbed watches until the Lazarus effect kicked in. There was joy in knowing a person would survive, but there was also a challenge in transitioning from a prolonged state of distress to one of normalcy. Those who had been ill resumed everyday acts that they'd previously abandoned, such as having their teeth cleaned and buying new clothes. But they also found themselves breaking off relationships where preparing for death had become a central reason for staying together.

Surviving was hard in other ways, too, particularly for those who had witnessed the greatest losses. "Like any war, you wonder why you came home," Peter Staley later observed. Survivor's guilt, it can be called, or, as Steve Bolerjack suggested in 2017, not necessarily guilt but "survivor's bafflement." Many people had barely had time to mourn because so many friends and loved ones had died for such a long time. It was particularly painful to consider the individuals who had died in the years just before the arrival of protease inhibitors and ART. If only they'd been able to hang on a little longer.

It wasn't just the infected who'd experienced the trauma of a pandemic. So had HIV-negative activists, family members of people with AIDS, and medical professionals who'd cared for patients. They'd all witnessed unnatural living and dying. "I remember their names," Los Angeles physician Michael Gottlieb recalled of his earliest cases during a 2016 retrospective about AIDS. "I remember what they looked like. I remember them in greater detail than patients I saw last week." "I miss so many people so bad," poet and feminist Dorothy Allison observed during a 1998 interview. Steve Bolerjack, whose record of dead friends grew to more than one hundred names at the height of the pandemic, occasionally still looks at his old list. "It jogs my memories, helps me remember people who are gone. But when I die, of course, those stories will disappear."

AIDS historian and activist David France has written about how, "An incomprehensible thing happens to the human mind when it is folded in fear and death for so long. It causes mysterious wounds and spurs unexplainable behaviors." Having gotten back their lives, many survivors went on to have them fall apart. They developed depression. They numbed old pains with alcohol and drugs. Crystal meth ensnared many survivors, including, for a time, TAG members Spencer Cox and Peter Staley. Some of the youngest activists and survivors had skipped normal phases of life development, such as going to college and pursuing careers. Fighting AIDS was what they'd done. That meant they'd missed the natural on-ramps for adulthood and didn't have self-sufficient patterns to fall back on.

Combination therapy presented its own challenges. It didn't take long for the HIV-positive to figure out that, even with new medications and ART, they would remain in a constant battle with the virus. "To proclaim that anyone with HIV is familiar with its four Ds (debilitation, depression, destitution, and death) is of course, gross understatement," wrote Bolerjack in a 2001 column he titled "HIV lite." "With the exception of actual death, most poz people contend with one of these factors every day."

Keeping ahead of HIV required so-called poz people (as in HIV-positive) to follow an intense regimen of care. Dozens of pills had to be taken with precision timing every day. HIV lay perpetually at the ready, waiting for a lapse in defenses, a chance to outwit a drug. Whenever it did, that medication could no longer be a part of the arsenal of potential weapons. Get too sloppy, and doctors ran out of options for keeping the virus at bay.

Stephen Gendin's death in 2000 at age thirty-four reinforced that point. Gendin had helped his friend Sean Strub found *POZ* magazine. He'd become widely known as a *POZ* writer and through his AIDS activism. Gendin had experimented aggressively with medication blending in the years leading up to ART, but his treatment plan may have backfired. His version of HIV seemed to have evolved until it could outsmart every possible drug combination, and he'd had a fatal heart attack while being treated for AIDS-related cancer.

Even when people were able to suppress the spread of HIV within their bodies, they faced countless troubling side effects. Some consequences were humbling, such as the way protease inhibitors sapped body fat away from desirable places, like the face and buttocks, and deposited it into what came to be known as Crix belly (named after the drug Crixivan) and protease paunch. This fat redistribution, known as lipodystrophy, was among the more benign side effects. Worse were the explosive bowel movements that came with almost no warning; those who experienced it have characterized it as projectile diarrhea.

Medications could cause nerve damage, elevate cholesterol levels, and put extra stress on organs such as the heart, liver, and kidneys. Before long, the pillboxes of the HIV-positive contained drugs for treating conditions caused by side effects of their HIV meds, and then medications that treated the side effects of the additional medicines.

The population of infected survivors became its own long-term study. Drug manufacturers had tested drugs to see if they worked, and they'd tested them for unrelated reactions. But no one knew what the substances might do to people who took them for decades. Nor did they anticipate all their unintended consequences. A reverse transcriptase inhibitor called Sustiva, for example, turned out to trigger suicide-inducing depression, especially among people already susceptible to dark moods. Dropping it from the pillbox literally pulled some people back from the brink of self-harm.

Living with HIV/AIDS took all the discipline, tolerance, awareness, and fortitude required for managing any chronic illness, but multiplied many times over. It also took a lot of money, particularly before the Affordable Care Act of 2010 made it illegal for health insurance providers to exclude potential customers from coverage because of preexisting medical conditions. Even for people lucky enough to have health insurance, navigating the system of deductions and benefits could be daunting. Finding and maintaining relationships with doctors, including those specializing in the long-term care of the HIV-positive, could be challenging, too. People with solid educations, financial reserves, and personal support systems in place held the best prospects for long-term survival. But for the many who didn't benefit from those resources, and especially for those who also faced the burdens of racism and poverty, managing HIV could be overwhelming.

Medical care was the core issue, but there were other challenges to living HIV-positive, too. Ongoing social stigma. The minefield of maintaining physical relationships in a world that judged the safety of sex by whether or not someone's lab results carried a plus sign or a minus mark after the letters *H-I-V*. The challenges of holding a job while managing a chronic illness. The risks of developing a major infection from someone else's everyday germs. And on and on and on.

It could be hard to rise from the dead.

▲

Even as the fight against HIV had intensified in the United States, the virus continued its march around the globe. Invariably, it gained an almost unshakable toehold before countries began to react. As it had in America, the virus struck marginalized and powerless segments of society first. Hemophiliacs in Japan. Prostitutes in Thailand. Intravenous drug users in Russia. It exploited the most vulnerable, and then spread from there.

HIV hitchhiked with truck drivers who visited brothels along the long-haul routes of Africa and India. It traveled with marauding soldiers in war-torn regions of Africa. It accompanied migrant work-

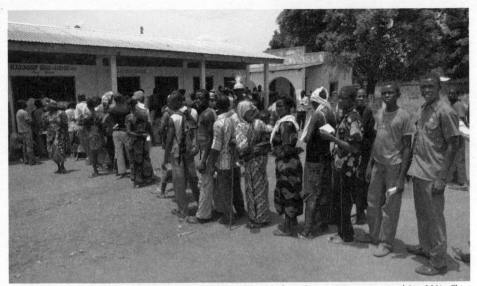

Residents of Bossangoa in the Central African Republic assemble for voluntary HIV testing, April 14, 2014. This country is one of many actively working to identify, contain, and treat infections in order to prevent the spread of HIV and reduce AIDS-related fatalities.

ers as they followed seasonal work across borders. Wherever it went, by the time leaders realized that other segments of the population were at risk, the virus had spread so widely that it seemed virtually impossible to extinguish.

Religious and cultural conservativism slowed response overseas, as they had in the United States. Political and regional instabilities also made it hard for some foreign governments to mount treatment and prevention programs, as did poverty in the developing world. By 2016, thirty-five years into the pandemic, more than 35 million people around the globe were living with HIV/AIDS. An equivalent number had died since the outbreak's emergence in 1981.

Late in the twentieth century, various international efforts to combat HIV began to coalesce behind a United Nations effort known as UNAIDS. The move reflected a growing realization that the virus wasn't just an international health threat; it posed a threat to global security, too. At the beginning of the twenty-first century, an international public/private initiative known as the Global Fund to Fight AIDS, Tuberculosis and Malaria was created to serve as a key fundraising source for UNAIDS. The United States became a major contributor to the fund starting in 2004 through a program known as PEPFAR—the President's Emergency Plan for AIDS Relief.

PEPFAR began during the presidency of George W. Bush, the son of the man who was living in the White House during the first Ashes Action. It has continued under subsequent administrations, and Congress has appropriated billions of dollars toward the international effort. These funds have supported efforts to train healthcare workers, conduct HIV testing, counsel people who are HIV-positive, prevent the transmission of HIV during pregnancy, and underwrite the costs of providing medications to impoverished populations.

PEPFAR, the Global Fund, and UNAIDS have had a tremendous impact on curtailing the spread of HIV and saving lives. More than half of the world's HIV-positive population now receives combination therapy, and prevention programs have begun to slow the spread of the virus around many parts of the globe. Efforts are now underway to expand that work until 90 percent of the world's infected population has been identified and is being successfully treated to the point of viral suppression. Should these goals be achieved by 2020, researchers predict an outcome for 2030 that was once considered unimaginable:

An end to the AIDS pandemic.

CHAPTER 15

LEGACIES

WHEN AIDS arrived on the scene in the 1980s, researchers and public health officials expected to develop a vaccine that would protect others from the spread of HIV. "We hope to have such a vaccine ready for testing in about two years," Health and Human Services director Margaret Heckler had boldly predicted in 1984. Yet no efforts then or in the decades since have succeeded. HIV presents a much tougher challenge than viral infections such as smallpox and polio. Vaccines worked on those infections because they could mimic the natural human immune response to the invading virus. Because the human body is unable to mount a successful response to HIV, there is no obvious way to build immunity to it through a vaccine.

"With other viruses, nature tells us just follow me and I'll lead you to a vaccine," observed Anthony Fauci in 2009 as part of his continuing oversight of HIV/AIDS research at the National Institutes of Health. "With HIV, nature is telling us if you follow me, you're going to be in trouble. We're going to have to push the envelope with HIV vaccinology in ways that we never had to do

Anthony Fauci speaks during an HIV/AIDS retrospective symposium at Cold Springs Harbor Laboratory, New York, October 2016. Fauci continues to direct NIH research related to the pandemic.

before. I feel that as we probe the scientific secrets of HIV, we may get there."

In addition to looking into the future, researchers have paused at times to evaluate their past. "We have to make sure the next generation in particular will have the history in mind for HIV and other diseases," observed Françoise Barré-Sinoussi, one of the Nobel Prize–winning virologists from the Pasteur Institute. "The next generation should not make the same mistakes," she told other research veterans during a 2016 symposium. "We're still in the midst of an epidemic," US retrovirologist David Baltimore observed at the same conference. He and others have maintained their study of HIV for decades in search of additional ways to control or eliminate the virus.

The most dramatic example of what amounts to an AIDS cure occurred this century for Timothy Ray Brown, otherwise known as the Berlin patient because that is where doctors reversed his infection with HIV. They did so during a bone marrow transplant for fighting leukemia, choosing a donor whose suitability included a beneficial genetic glitch. A small percentage of humans lack one of the two receptors required for HIV to attach successfully to CD4 cells. Their immune system functions normally otherwise, but the lack of the second receptor provides the added bonus of preventing infection from HIV.

In 2007, after two transplant attempts, Brown became not just cancer-free—he was HIV-free, too. His immune system had adopted the same mutation as his donor's, leaving the virus no way to perpetuate itself in his body. Bone marrow transplants are such complex and grueling procedures that they wouldn't be a practical form of treatment for all people living with HIV/AIDS. But the science behind them may lead to less arduous ways of disabling the actions of CD4 receptors or otherwise altering the body's defenses, including through genetic engineering.

▲

Scientific research has not only helped us understand how to study HIV going forward; it has also filled holes in the virus's historical past. Earlier this century researchers finally traced the pandemic's point of origin to events that occurred more than a century ago in the region of southeastern Cameroon in Central Africa. Someone— probably a monkey hunter—became infected with the HIV virus by having blood-on-blood contact with an infected chimpanzee. This sort of cross-species spillover of viruses is not unusual; plenty of similar transfers have occurred. But most of those transfers didn't become pandemics for a variety of reasons, including the isolation of individual communities. HIV spillovers were particularly prone to fade because it can take a long time for an HIV-positive person to reach the end stages of AIDS. People who carried the virus and those they passed it to probably died from other, more immediate causes, forcing the virus to die out rather than spread in contagion.

The virus finally did take hold on the African continent about 1908 after someone, perhaps an infected Cameroonian traveler, carried the virus to more populous areas. After HIV reached the Congolese city of Brazzaville and the neighboring city now known as Kinshasa in Central Africa, it spread even faster until dozens and then hundreds carried the virus. An act of goodwill probably led to the inadvertent spread of HIV beyond Africa. In the early 1960s, many Haitians had answered a call for staffing help in the newly independent Republic of Congo. Hundreds crossed the Atlantic to serve as doctors, nurses, educators, lawyers, and public administrators. Around 1967, when they began to return home, at least one of them unwittingly carried HIV to the Americas. Back in Haiti, this individual, and perhaps others, passed the virus along to sexual partners.

During the late 1960s or early 1970s at least one infected person must have donated plasma in the Haitian capital, Port-au-Prince, inadvertently introducing HIV into the center's supply of blood plasma. Such donations also spread the infection to other donors through a design flaw in the plasma collection machine. This forensic history helps explain why Haitian Americans had inexplicably been some of the first people to exhibit symptoms of infection at the beginning of the epidemic. HIV's leap from Haiti to the nearby United States in about 1971 was relatively easy. Either it arrived in a contaminated unit of Haitian blood plasma, or it hitchhiked to America via an infected traveler. The virus reached New York City first, but by 1976 HIV had crossed the country and begun spreading in San Francisco, as well.

Research has solved other disputes about AIDS, too. It debunked the claim that something other than HIV was causing AIDS. The rationale for this increasingly controversial idea collapsed after combination therapy proved how effectively it could control the syndrome. Researchers also discredited the longstanding rumor that federal researchers had developed AIDS in the pursuit of germ warfare agents. This idea had been planted during a disinformation campaign by the former Soviet Union in an effort to promote public distrust of the United States government.

In 2016 scientists announced that genetic mapping of the evolution of HIV had disproved the portrayal of Gaëtan Dugas as the infamous Patient Zero. The idea that Dugas had served as the vector for the rampant spread of HIV took hold through Randy Shilts's 1987 history of AIDS, *And the Band Played On*, a work that not only vilified Dugas but also originated the use of the Patient Zero phrase. Dugas's career as a Canadian flight attendant and his admissions of widespread sexual promiscuity provided convincing circumstantial evidence of culpability. So, seemingly, did his designation as Patient O on a CDC map of early AIDS cases. Rather than standing for zero, though, the map used the letter O to indicate that Dugas, unlike other patients, resided outside the map's zone of infection. It took until 2016 to identify that error and for genetic research to prove that Dugas, who died from AIDS in 1984 at age thirty-one, could not possibly have started the contagion.

▲

Even as researchers put old rumors to rest, HIV continues to spread the same way it always did—by ignorance and carelessness. The learning curve on AIDS begins anew with each generation. Those born in recent decades have no memory of the horrifying force with which HIV hit the United States and the world. Others dismiss the risks of infection, perhaps assuming, wrongly, that by making HIV/AIDS treatable scientists have made it easy to live with. It doesn't help that sexual intercourse is by its very nature an emotional act; safety-conscious intentions may be set aside during a moment of passion, prompting an instance of unprotected sex with life-altering consequences.

And yet, as longtime survivor Sean Strub warned, "You don't want to get this virus. It's a lifelong health challenge, it's expensive, it's time-consuming, it's stigmatizing beyond belief, and it complicates intimate relationships in ways one can't possibly understand unless they've gone through it."

The treatment regimen remains so daunting that only about half of HIV-positive Americans manage to keep the virus completely under control. For those who do, "You live or die by the pillbox," reminded Steve Bolerjack. Access to health insurance has improved, but the cost of care remains expensive, about $50 per day, which amounts to hundreds of thousands of dollars over a lifetime.

More than 700,000 Americans have died because of AIDS since the pandemic began, and more than 1 million people in the United States are living with HIV/AIDS. Each year as many as 40,000 people in the country learn that they are HIV-positive, but the CDC estimates that about 150,000 people are unaware of being infected. Many are teenagers and young adults. In consequence, people continue to unwittingly pass HIV to others, just as they have for more than a century.

Although everyone remains vulnerable to infection, the virus continues to strike an unequal path through society. People of color account for almost three-quarters of new cases every year. About half of new infections occur in the South, and twenty-one of the top twenty-five metropolitan areas where gay and bisexual men are at greatest risk of infection are southern. Florida is home to an estimated half of the nation's HIV-positive population. The concentration of HIV has become so high in some communities that it can be hard to avoid the virus, and yet these same population centers often lack the activist networks and resources required to counter the trends. Without increased prevention and treatment

Earvin "Magic" Johnson participates in a discussion about HIV/AIDS, April 30, 2008. The basketball legend has advocated for prevention and treatment programs since learning that he was HIV-positive in 1991.

efforts, gay and bisexual black men in the United States face a 50 percent chance of becoming HIV-positive in their lifetimes, putting them at a higher risk of infection than citizens from any other part of the world.

HIV continues to spread predominantly by sexual intercourse, particularly among gay and bisexual partners; these populations account for 70 percent of annual infections. Only about a quarter of those infected in a given year are heterosexuals. Intravenous drug users remain a relatively small but consistently vulnerable group, accounting for fewer than 10 percent of annual infections. Almost a quarter of all those diagnosed with HIV are between the ages of thirteen and twenty-four. A significant number of infections also take place among people over fifty; typically this age group accounts for about 15 percent of annual infections.

One of the best ways to stop HIV is through widespread testing, treatment, and the adoption of precautions to prevent the further spread of infection. Efforts that encourage testing can be undercut in states where it is illegal to conceal being HIV-positive. Individuals can be prosecuted for hiding their status, and those who are convicted can be branded as felons and sex offenders. To evade punishment, people at risk of being HIV-positive may avoid testing; it's easier to plead innocence when there's no existing lab work.

Criminalizing the concealment of one's HIV status contributes to the disproportionate representation of HIV/AIDS in the nation's prison population and its further spread behind prison walls. Rates of infection are five times higher among incarcerated people than for those not in the criminal justice system.

Many of the best defenses against HIV today are the same ones used in past decades—wearing condoms, using clean needles, or working with needle exchanges—but new methods exist, too. Women can reduce their risk of infection even without their partner's assistance by using female condoms, a protective device that lines the vaginal walls, or by inserting microbicide gel into the vagina before and after sexual intercourse. Mother-to-child transmission of HIV dropped dramatically in the United States and around the world after doctors discovered that HIV-positive women who take modest doses of AZT during pregnancy are less likely to transmit the virus to a child in utero. The continued use of this strategy has all but eliminated what was once a significant pathway for the spread of infection.

Members of high-risk populations, particularly men who have sex with men, can defend themselves against HIV by taking a small daily dose of antiretroviral medication. This therapy, which became available in 2012, is known as pre-exposure prophylaxis, or PrEP, and by the brand name Truvada. Using condoms at the same time as PrEP provides additional protection. In cases where sexual assault or a comparable emergency puts someone at an unexpected risk of HIV exposure, physicians and emergency room doctors can prescribe a course of treatment known as PEP (short for post-exposure prophylaxis). Such treatment must be started within three days to be effective.

In recent years researchers have determined that well-regulated adherence to combination therapy regimens helps to limit the reach of the virus, too. ART can decrease the presence of HIV in someone's body so successfully that there is not enough surviving virus left for it to spread to another person. Such a circumstance decreases viral transmission within what are called serodiscordant relationships, where one partner is HIV-positive and the other is HIV-negative. People in these relationships can further reduce the chance of infection by employing such preventive measures as condoms and PrEP.

Intravenous drug users remain at risk of contracting HIV depending on their access to clean needles. Despite the fact that the CDC began recommending needle exchanges as a harm reduction strategy in 1984, government rules prohibit the use of federal funds for them, falling back on false arguments that they promote illegal behavior. Nonetheless, more than two-thirds of states have needle exchanges in selected areas; all depend on state, local, or nongovernmental sources of funds. Sometimes it takes a crisis for policies to change. Such was the case during 2015 in southeastern Indiana where a massive spike in HIV infections prompted the state's conservative governor to allow affected areas to establish exchanges.

Ironically it costs far more to care for people with HIV/AIDS than it would cost to help them avoid infection in the first place via needle exchanges and prevention efforts. Annually the US government devotes more than $30 billion to matters involving HIV/AIDS. About 65 percent of that sum goes to the nation's domestic care and treatment programs. Almost 10 percent provides housing assistance and other cash subsidies. Approximately 7 percent supports research-related programs, and another 2 percent funds education and prevention efforts domestically. The rest goes to international efforts related to research, care, and prevention through such programs as PEPFAR.

▲

Long-term HIV-positive survivors of the AIDS pandemic are approaching their sixties, seventies, and even eighties, a prospect that was unthinkable at the height of the crisis. For all the benefits of an extended lifespan, these individuals face more complications than peers who are HIV-negative. They're more likely to develop cancer and cardiovascular disease; they're at greater risk of financial stress; and they're more likely to be isolated and suffer from depression.

Even the aging process itself is faster for those who've spent decades living with HIV/AIDS. Earlier arthritis. Poorer memory skills. Declining mobility. "I'm a young old man," observed Scott Jordan in 2013 at age fifty-two. Decades of toxic medications make long-term survivors more prone to organ failures, which in and of itself can become a death sentence. Lawmakers helped to address this challenge during Barack Obama's administration by approving the sharing of organs between HIV-positive people, something previously prohibited.

Maintaining mental health may be one of the greatest challenges faced by long-term survivors of HIV/AIDS. Beyond the stress of the physical issues and financial worries that come with a chronic illness, beyond the loneliness that everyone faces as they age, there are the scars of having survived what amounted to a plague. Many still bear wounds from the fight that claimed friends, loved ones, and the promises of a generation. And these veterans of HIV/AIDS continue to live with a heightened threat of loss. The partner whose medications failed—because that can still happen. The worry that their own regimen might fail and that a new one won't be found fast enough to save their life. The friend who got tired of the work of staying well, quit taking meds, and died.

Pill fatigue, some call it. Friends suspect that's what claimed the life of Spencer Cox, whose health declined with unexpected speed before his death in 2012 at age forty-four. Cox had been the member of TAG who conceived the strategy that expedited the development of combination therapy. He had literally saved thousands of lives through his activism, yet his own life was cut short. The bitter irony of his death shook ACT UP and TAG survivors particularly hard.

So had the loss a few years earlier of another icon from the AIDS activist movement, Rodger McFarlane. McFarlane was the gay liberation veteran who went on to revolutionize the care for people with AIDS at Gay Men's Health Crisis and other organizations. McFarlane himself had escaped HIV infection, crediting, he figured, "some genetic little glitch that went my way." AIDS didn't kill him, but it had to have taken a toll. As he aged and realized his own health would likely require the help of others, the man who had turned care into an art form and a profession chose not to be on the receiving end of the process. In 2009, at age fifty-four, he took his own life.

Deaths such as Cox's and McFarlane's provide occasions for old friends to reunite and reflect on how AIDS changed their lives. Peter Staley spoke to that fact during Cox's memorial service in 2013. "While many of us, through luck or circumstance, have landed on our feet, all of us, in some way, have unprocessed grief, or guilt, or an overwhelming sense of abandonment from a community that turned its back on us and increasingly stigmatized us, all in an attempt to pretend that AIDS wasn't a problem anymore."

Bob Rafsky holds his eighteen-month-old daughter Sara, 1987. Rafsky died at age forty-seven from HIV/AIDS in 1993 when Sara was seven years old.

The wounds from what Garance Franke-Ruta has character-ized as a "collective mass death experience" can run broad as well as deep. They don't just linger among HIV-positive survivors; they continue to affect their allies, friends, and family members, too. "For 20 years, I battled my grief in the shadows," recalled Sara Rafsky, who lost her father, Bob Rafsky, when she was a young girl. In recent years she and other now-grown children of deceased par-ents have found one another and created a network of peer allies known as the Recollectors.

Sara Rafsky began meeting her father's old friends from ACT UP when their paths crossed at the premiere of David France's 2012 film *How to Survive a Plague*, a documentary that was interspersed with home movie clips of her childhood interactions with her par-ents. The meeting was mutually affecting. "I had all this history with Bob Rafsky," Peter Staley noted, and then, "All of a sudden, here was his beautiful adult daughter. She looked so much like him. She knew him as a father, but not an activist. I could tell her about that part of his life." Sara Rafsky has come to see the discovery of her father's old comrades as akin to finding long-lost uncles.

In 2015 a group of ACT UP veterans gathered in New York City to meet and support the stories shared by Rafsky and other Recollectors. The aging activists were, according to a *Times* reporter, "beaming like proud parents." Such meetings have allowed this younger generation of survivors to break through a barrier that likewise constrained their parents: silence. "One of the things that brings the Recollectors together is how we suffered from the closet more than we suffered from the disease," observed Marco Roth. His father, a physician, died from AIDS after becoming infected through his work when Roth was a teenager.

▲

Although it can be tempting to assess HIV/AIDS in numbers—the numbers of the dead, the numbers of the infected, the numbers who will die this year, and the next, and beyond—the legacy of the pandemic extends beyond those measures. HIV and AIDS changed the United States itself in ways that have been substantial, lasting, and, not infrequently, for the better.

The LGBTQ community formed an unshakable and highly visible alliance in response to AIDS, an alliance that became the engine for so much social progress.

The decriminalization of homosexuality.

Marriage equality.

Health insurance for people with preexisting conditions.

The Affordable Care Act and its promise of universal healthcare—the affirmation that healthcare is a right.

All of these innovations owe their roots to the AIDS pandemic. So do peer-based care initiatives, patients' rights movements, and the growth of health advocacy fund-raising. AIDS revolutionized healthcare itself, in everything from how to protect the nation's blood supply, to the wearing of protective masks and gloves by medical practitioners and first responders, to procedures for testing new medications. AIDS altered the ways that people prepare for their deaths. Healthcare directives, hospice care, morphine drips, and physician-assisted suicides all took widespread root during the pandemic. Even a loop of thin red ribbon, which people began pinning to their clothes during 1991 as a sign of solidarity in the fight against HIV/AIDS, became a token that would be used for other causes in other colors.

One of the most enduring reminders of the impact HIV had on humanity is the AIDS memorial quilt. Through the decades it has grown to more than 48,000 panels. The deaths it commemorates have come in varied waves. The first was predominantly white and gay. Early panels sometimes withheld last names, reflecting how closeted the era remained. Full names followed. Then panels began to memorialize African Americans and other people of color, as well. The quilt grew with the pandemic, expanding early on by 11,000 panels in a single year. Today, on average its curators receive one new panel a day. Cindy "Gert" McMullin, one of the project's original volunteers, turned thirty-two the year the quilt began. Now in her sixties, she continues to keep the memorial in repair and helps it grow by guiding new panels through the sewing machine that stitches together each commemorative block.

Cleve Jones, whose inspiration and actions gave birth to the quilt, is an activist, not an archivist, so the care for the quilt has become the work of its associated NAMES Foundation under the direction of Julie Rhoad in Atlanta, Georgia. "The quilt is the most democratic memorial ever made," Rhoad has noted, calling it "the largest piece of ongoing folk art in the world." Although the fifty-four-ton quilt has not been exhibited in its entirety since 1996, blocks are on constant rotation for display at sites around the United States and beyond, particularly during the annual observance of World AIDS Day, December 1.

The AIDS memorial quilt may be the largest and most visible example of the pandemic's commemoration, but countless personal remembrances endure for the people who survived HIV's deadly march. There are the handwritten lists, the aging stacks of Rolo-dead cards, analog address books with crossed-out entries, and cherished photographs of memories made when everyone was healthy and thought their whole lives were ahead of them.

Poster urging participation in weekly ACT UP meetings, circa 1993.

Garance Franke-Ruta considered becoming a doctor because of her experiences with ACT UP and TAG. Instead she became a journalist. In 2013 she wrote a retrospective about her involvement for the *Atlantic* magazine and concluded it with a memorial list of key ACT UP members lost to AIDS. It ran to more than one hundred names. "Every person who lived through those years in certain communities knows they can compile a list like this one, if they have not already, and if they can bear it," she wrote. Seeing the names serves as a reminder, she observed.

"There was a time when we were all alive together."

EPILOGUE

"BURY me furiously," Mark Lowe Fisher had instructed his friends before he died from AIDS in 1992. "We are not just spiraling statistics," he wrote. "We are people who have lives, who have purpose, who have lovers, friends and families. And we are dying of a disease maintained by a degree of criminal neglect so enormous that it amounts to genocide. . . . I want my own funeral to be fierce and defiant."

Thus, on the rainy afternoon of November 2, 1992, the day before the nation elected its first Democratic president since the arrival of AIDS, his friends gathered beside his open coffin and began to march. They processed thirty-nine blocks from lower Manhattan to the Midtown reelection headquarters of George H. W. Bush, walking alongside Fisher's body as the darkness of evening slowly settled over the city. Then they stood together in the rain-soaked street and honored Fisher's parting wish.

Bob Rafsky, who knew by then he was dying from AIDS, spoke to the somber crowd. "Let everyone here know, that this is not a political funeral for Mark Fisher," he said. "It's a political funeral for the man who killed him and so many others and is slowly killing me, whose name curls my tongue and curls my breath. George Bush, we believe you'll be defeated tomorrow because we believe there's still some justice left in the universe and some compassion left in the American people."

Rafsky cursed the president while others tried to shield the body of their dead friend from the falling rain. He continued: "When the living can no longer speak, the dead may speak for them. Mark's voice is here with us." Rafsky, his own voice rising, implored, "Let the whole earth hear us now: We beg, we pray, we demand that this epidemic end, not just so we may live, but so that Mark's soul may rest in peace at last." Then, in solemn tones, he closed his remarks with a battle cry that echoes still:

"In anger and in grief, this fight is not over until all of us are safe.

"Act up.

"Fight back.

"Fight AIDS."

Twenty years after the Stonewall riots, this ACT UP mailing called for a new riot to push back against injustices faced by the LGBTQ community, minorities, and women during the height of the HIV/AIDS crisis, 1989. For many, the fight continues.

A NOTE FROM THE AUTHOR

Because the story of HIV/AIDS is too big for one book, I have written the volume I was meant to write. I have deliberately chosen to focus on the bleakest years of the American struggle, 1981 to 1996, in part because I am of the same generation as so many whose lives were unnaturally cut short. I wrote particularly about them because I want those who passed so early and too soon to be remembered for their suffering, their dying, and, most importantly, for their living.

I moved to New York City in 1979, fresh from college and at the height of the city's gay sexual revolution. It was impossible not to sense the liberating electricity that pulsed through an area such as Greenwich Village, and I've tried to capture that feeling in my writing. Ironically, I left New York the same week that the *New York Times* published its Fourth of July story about peculiar medical symptoms clustered in gay men. When I returned to visit the city in subsequent years, the joyful vibe I remembered from Christopher Street had given way to a palpable gloom of grief and darkness. That sense memory helped to fuel my research and writing choices, too.

Since I have elected to concentrate on this time span, the resulting book focuses by necessity on the impact of HIV/AIDS on gay men in general, and white gay men particularly. More than 70 percent of the earliest cases of the syndrome were among men having sex with men. White gay men still constituted the majority of the infected as we neared the era of lifesaving medications in the mid-1990s, but by then infections among people of color were on the rise.

This book continues the examination of LGBTQ history I began with *Stonewall: Breaking Out in the Fight for Gay Rights*. When I started my work on *Stonewall*, I had no idea that it would lead me to a new project. But I found it supremely difficult to stop researching *Stonewall*'s single chapter about AIDS, and I knew I wanted to explore the subject further. Only later, as I waded deeper and deeper into the topic, did I begin to question my thinking. How in the world would I be able to wrap my arms around such a lengthy and complex history without squeezing the life out of it? And how would I immerse myself in such a dark period without being overwhelmed by the gloom?

Over and over I found myself meeting courageous, funny, and memorable activists through the pages of history, only to discover the disease had killed them. It was dark work. And yet, during the many months while I lived in my head in that era, the people I'd come to care about seemed very much alive. After my work finished and the historical figures I'd breathed life into were gone all over again, my sorrow returned. Perhaps, in consolation, these individuals will likewise come alive, at least fleetingly, for those who read this book.

In January 2017 I visited the AIDS memorial quilt in Atlanta. We tend to picture the quilt as it appears when it is on display. I wanted to see it at rest. Julie Rhoad was kind enough to welcome me to the modest headquarters for the NAMES Foundation and to walk me through the aisles of shelves and bins holding quilt blocks. Each section was carefully labeled with numbers that corresponded to records for tracing the location of individual panels. At one point I asked Rhoad how she could work in the company of so much sadness and grief. She paused, then surprised me by replying, "We're not surrounded by sadness. We're surrounded by love."

When I began this book, I knew the subject matter would almost invariably become heavy and disheartening. It can be hard to face the pre-ART loss of almost a half-million fellow Americans, not to mention the millions of people around the planet who have died because of HIV/AIDS. "I'm working up my courage to bear the history," I wrote in my journal as I prepared to dive deeper into the story of the pandemic. Yet even as I researched the nation's halting response to the crisis, even as I wrote about the deaths of people I had come to admire, even as I shed tears, even then, I did not falter.

As the book neared completion I realized the source of that resolve. It wasn't grief. It wasn't anger—although I certainly felt that often enough. It wasn't even my sheer determination to complete the task. Throughout the project I was surrounded by a force that became stronger with time and grew thanks to connections and kinships forged with friends and strangers alike. A force that moves with the stealth and power of a virus, but with a far different effect. A force that may be the most powerful one of all.

Love.

ACKNOWLEDGMENTS

So many individuals helped me during the course of this project. Some names carry back to the work I did for *Stonewall: Breaking Out in the Fight for Gay Rights*, including help I received from Tal Nadan at the Manuscripts and Archives Division of the New York Public Library and Rich Wandel at the National History Archive of the LGBT Community Center in New York City. Both institutions and curators contributed materials that helped me make not only that first book but also this second one, for which I remain very grateful. I likewise appreciate the institutions and individuals who contributed photographs and illustrations to this book, all of whom are gratefully acknowledged on p. 164.

The accompanying bibliography acknowledges the most notable sources I consulted in the course of researching this history. A more complete bibliography may be found at my author website. I am particularly indebted to the authors of several books that proved invaluable to my work. These titles include *AIDS at 30* by Victoria A. Harden, the founding director of the Office of NIH History, a post she held through much of the AIDS pandemic; science writer David Quammen's book *The Chimp and the River*, which helped me understand the origins of AIDS as well as HIV; and the documentation by eyewitnesses to history, including Sean Strub's memoir *Body*

Counts, the book and film by David France that share the title *How to Survive a Plague*, and the works of other documentary filmmakers. Such works provide an invaluable resource about a pandemic that has otherwise cut living memory unnaturally short.

My friend and fellow author Sue Macy directed my attention on countless occasions to resources and exhibits of interest. She is the source of my understanding of Scholastic's educational outreach efforts during the 1990s, having shared a box of samples collected during her years of work with this publisher. My friends Curt Deane and Tom Shoemaker likewise shared tips and connections; I remain particularly indebted to Tom for the introduction he made to Steve Bolerjack. Steve, a columnist for the *New York Blade* in the 1990s and early 2000s, enriched my understanding of both the history of the pandemic and the world of living HIV-positive through his writings and our conversations. He also directed me toward helpful resources that I might not otherwise have found.

I'm additionally grateful to Steve for his careful reading of this book in manuscript form, and to Marion Field Fass, professor emerita of biology and health and society at Beloit College, for her own perceptive review. Both Steve and Marion have strengthened the book immeasurably in consequence. Thank you! I'm also indebted to Beloit College intern Mariah Cadwallader for her enthusiasm and valuable assistance during the initial phase of this book's research.

I remain grateful to my publisher at Viking, Ken Wright, not only for helping me bring *Stonewall* to life but for embracing immediately and enthusiastically my suggestion that we collaborate on a second title about LGBTQ history. Ken deserves additional credit for introducing me to my project editor for both books, Catherine Frank, and to his superb team of production and marketing colleagues at Penguin Random House. As was the case in the past, Catherine's editorial guidance has strengthened every page of this manuscript, as is surely true for all others she shepherds into print. I am fortunate to work with her and so many other fine stewards of the published word, including Sheila Keenan, Jody Corbett, Laura Stiers, Janet B. Pascal, Abigail Powers, Krista Ahlberg, and Marinda Valenti. Kate Renner brought the text to life with her vibrant design, working in coordination with art director Denise Cronin. The Penguin Young Readers sales and marketing teams have assured that the book finds appreciative readers. I'm grateful to the creative talents of Listening Library for rendering the book so expertly into audio form.

My critique group lost a longtime member during the making of this book, and I grieved the passing of Elizabeth Fixmer even as I went to work every day to read and write about death. Elizabeth gladdened this load through her example of embracing the potential for living, right down to her final days of friendship and storytelling. I am fortunate to continue to share our writing journey with fellow critique partners Pam Beres, Georgia Beaverson, Judy Bryan, and Jamie A. Swenson.

My loving and incredibly tolerant friends and family have miraculously survived the making of another book, including my inevitable disappearances for research and periods of writing hibernation. Thank you for being there whenever I come out of my den, including nearby friends Kedron Wiersgalla, Hester White, and Peggy Maiken; friends scattered farther afield; my ever-engaged nonagenarian parents, Dolores and Henry; my steadfast brother, David, and sister-in-law, Mary; and, always, always, the pair of children who led me to write books in the first place but who are now fully grown men, my sons, Jake and Sam.

Thank you, thank you, one and all.

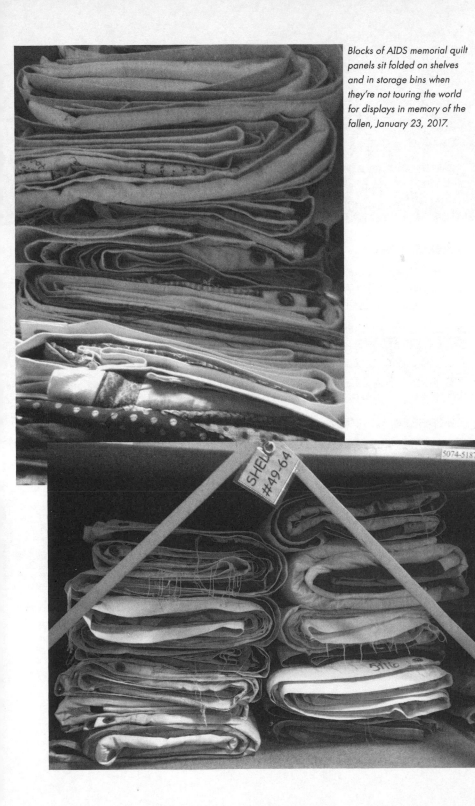

Blocks of AIDS memorial quilt panels sit folded on shelves and in storage bins when they're not touring the world for displays in memory of the fallen, January 23, 2017.

KEY EVENTS IN THE HISTORY OF AIDS IN AMERICA, 1981-1997

JUNE 5, 1981

The first of three early notices about the illness that will become known as HIV/AIDS appear in the *MMWR* weekly newsletter of the Centers for Disease Control (CDC).

AUGUST 11, 1981

Larry Kramer hosts an informal fund-raiser and informational session about the mysterious outbreak at his New York apartment.

DECEMBER 10, 1981

Bobbi Campbell takes on the role of KS Poster Boy in an effort to raise awareness in San Francisco about the mysterious rise of infection among gay men.

JANUARY 4, 1982

Larry Kramer and other gay men found Gay Men's Health Crisis (GMHC) in New York City.

SEPTEMBER 24, 1982

After infections emerge beyond the gay community, the CDC replaces GRID (gay-related immune deficiency) with the term AIDS, acronym for what becomes known as acquired immunodeficiency syndrome.

MARCH 1983

The CDC warns that AIDS may be spreading via sexual intercourse and contact with infected blood and blood products. It asks members of high-risk groups to stop donating blood.

MAY 18, 1983

Congress passes its first AIDS-specific funding allocation, $12 million.

MAY 20, 1983

Researchers at the Pasteur Institute in Paris report that they have identified a new virus and suggest it could be causing AIDS. The pathogen eventually becomes known as the human immunodeficiency virus, or HIV.

JUNE 1983

Eleven symptomatic gay men form People with AIDS and unveil its eleven founding tenets. These so-called Denver Principles guide the evolving treatment protocol for infected individuals.

MARCH 2, 1985

The Food and Drug Administration (FDA) approves a blood-screening test for HIV, prompting blood banks to begin screening the nation's blood supply.

JULY 25, 1985

The public learns that Rock Hudson has AIDS.

AUGUST 27, 1985

Indiana student Ryan White draws national attention after his local public school bans the HIV-positive hemophiliac from attending classes.

SEPTEMBER 17, 1985

President Ronald Reagan makes his first public reference to AIDS since the syndrome appeared in 1981. More than eighteen months pass before he delivers his first speech about the epidemic.

DECEMBER 1985

By the end of the year, HIV had spread to every region of the planet, making it a worldwide pandemic.

OCTOBER 22, 1986

The surgeon general of the United States calls for increased nationwide public awareness about HIV/AIDS.

FEBRUARY 1987

Cleve Jones and a friend make the first panels for the AIDS memorial quilt. Eight months later the quilt is displayed for the first time on the National Mall in Washington, DC.

MARCH 12, 1987

Larry Kramer and others found the AIDS Coalition to Unleash Power (ACT UP) in New York City. They hold their first demonstration twelve days later.

MARCH 19, 1987

The medication known as AZT goes on sale for use in the treatment of AIDS.

MAY 1988

Every household in the United States receives a mailed brochure from the surgeon general as part of his educational campaign about HIV/AIDS.

OCTOBER 11, 1988

ACT UP stages its Seize Control of the FDA protest over the Food and Drug Administration's slow approval of drugs.

DECEMBER 10, 1989

ACT UP mounts its Stop the Church protest during Sunday service at St. Patrick's Cathedral in New York.

MAY 21, 1990

ACT UP holds its Storm the NIH protest over the federal government's slow response to the AIDS pandemic.

NOVEMBER 1991

A group of members from ACT UP's Treatment + Data affinity group (T+D) break away to form the Treatment Action Group (TAG).

NOVEMBER 7, 1991

Magic Johnson announces he is HIV-positive and ends his professional basketball career with the Los Angeles Lakers.

OCTOBER 11, 1992

ACT UP protests the presidency of George H. W. Bush through its Ashes Action.

DECEMBER 1995

The first protease inhibitor drug reaches the market, and two more go on sale the following March. These medications usher in the era of highly active antiretroviral therapy, or HAART, and later, ART.

1997

Thanks to ART the rate of death from AIDS in America declines for the first time since the emergence of AIDS in 1981.

ADDITIONAL RESOURCES

ACT UP Oral History Project
http://www.actuporalhistory.org/interviews/index.html

AIDS Coalition to Unleash Power (ACT UP)
http://www.actupny.org/

amfAR, the Foundation for AIDS Research
https://www.amfar.org/thirty-years-of-hiv/aids-snapshots-of-an-epidemic/

Elizabeth Glaser Pediatric AIDS Foundation
http://www.pedaids.org/

Gay Men's Health Crisis (GMHC)
gmhc.org/

The Global Fund
https://www.theglobalfund.org/en/

HIV.gov
https://www.hiv.gov/

How to Survive a Plague
https://surviveaplague.com/resources

Magic Johnson Foundation HIV/AIDS Initiatives
http://magicjohnson.org/programs/hivaids-initiatives/

POZ
https://www.poz.com

The Recollectors
therecollectors.com/

The Sero Project
http://www.seroproject.com/

The Stigma Project
blog.thestigmaproject.org/

Treatment Action Group (TAG)
treatmentactiongroup.org/

UNAIDS
http://www.unaids.org/en

SOURCE NOTES

PROLOGUE
"He has slimming disease . . .": Harden, 8.

PART ONE—CONTAGION
"Too much is being transmitted . . .": Shilts, 40.

CHAPTER 1—BEFORE
"All of those loves that dare not speak . . .": *Gay Sex in the 70s*.
"Come to Man's Country . . .": ibid.
"It was simple . . .": ibid.
"It was hard not to feel great love . . .": ibid.
"too much": Shilts, 40.
"We didn't know we were dancing on the edge . . . ": Dunlap, "As Disco Faces Razing, Gay Alumni Share Memories."

CHAPTER 2—OUTBREAK
"Unusual": "*Pneumocystis* pneumonia—Los Angeles."
"The sure sign of someone who's going to kick . . .": Folkart.
"Rare Cancer Seen in 41 Homosexuals." Altman, "Rare Cancer Seen in 41 Homosexuals."
"spent the long weekend examining one another's flesh": France, *How to Survive a Plague* (book), 14.
"I'm writing because I have . . .": Shilts, 108.

CHAPTER 3—REACTIONS
"I don't think anybody is . . .": France, *How to Survive a Plague* (book), 22.
"The poor homosexuals . . .": Buchanan.
"Sometimes the list is . . .": Strub, 174.
"We were forced to take care of ourselves . . .": Hevesi.
"the first case, I think, in history . . .": *Gay Sex in the 70s*.
"We know who we are . . .": Callen and Berkowitz.
"For us, the party that was the '70s is over.": ibid.
"merely the tip of the iceberg . . .": Harden, 36.
"the nail in the coffin": ibid, 31.

CHAPTER 4—BEARINGS
"If this article doesn't scare the shit out of you . . .": Kramer, "1,112 and Counting."
"If we don't act immediately . . .": ibid.
"I think it's the toughest issue we've yet faced." Craig Rodwell Papers (personal note from Toby Marotta).

"it is known to be fatal . . .": Harden, 88.

"Don't say there wasn't enough money": Daly.

"I don't say hope will guarantee you'll beat AIDS . . .": Dunlap, "Michael Callen, Singer and Expert On Coping With AIDS, Dies at 38."

"To die—and to LIVE—in dignity.": France, *How to Survive a Plague* (book), 110.

PART TWO—CATASTROPHE

"Someday, the AIDS crisis will be over . . .": Russo.

CHAPTER 5—OUTED

"Suddenly it was common to see . . .": Bolerjack, *Pride, Politics & Plague*, 42.

"Essentially we did two things . . .": ibid., 162.

"When I heard of someone who was sick . . .": Strub, 147.

"would not be assigned to cover AIDS." Harden, 99.

"Everybody is hysterical": Daly.

"Don't sleep with him . . . ": ibid.

"Any homosexual or Haitian has become an object of dread": ibid.

"Is the president concerned about this subject?" McKay.

"one of the top priorities": Ronald Reagan Presidential Library and Museum, news conference, September 17, 1985.

CHAPTER 6—POSITIVE

"Now no one is safe from AIDS"; "the new victims"; and "the AIDS minorities are beginning to infect . . .": Barnes and Hollister.

"Everybody was fearful . . . ": Bolerjack, interview with author, March 3, 2017.

"When I left [the doctor's] office, . . .": Strub, 165.

"At the time I was diagnosed, . . .": Ain.

"I didn't want to believe him": Earvin "Magic" Johnson, 275.

"When I think about that particular moment . . . ": *Absolutely Positive*.

"I'm having trouble accepting . . .": ibid.

"You find out this information and you're crushed . . .": ibid.

CHAPTER 7—TRANSITIONS

"you watched people die rapid, hard deaths . . .": Rhoad.

"People would go fast . . .": Sokol.

"Friday he had a fever . . .": France, *How to Survive a Plague* (book), 125.

"I can't do a lot of things anymore . . .": *Living with AIDS*.

"It's a hideous disease . . . ": Solomon.

"Well, gee, did I, do I really deserve this?": *Absolutely Positive*.

"How do you live in a room with a monster? . . .": ibid.

"I've always got to be spiritual . . .": ibid.

"By 1986, a third of the hospital's beds were filled . . .": Boynton.

"Several times, I went to the AIDS ward . . . ": Strub, 191.

"Steven, I have always loved you and . . .": Steven J. Powsner Papers, correspondence from
   Bruce Philip Cooper, December 18, 1986.
"Do you remember how we said . . .": Strub, 260.
"We personally witnessed the courage and grace . . .": ibid., 261.
"By the time you receive this letter . . .": ibid., 348–349.
"We were going to more funerals and memorial services . . .": ibid., 428.
"When you are sitting close to me . . .": ibid., 216.
"That's my Rolo-dead file.": ibid, 191.
"I'm an organized person and when it all started . . .": Bolerjack, interview with author,
   March 3, 2017.

CHAPTER 8—OUTRAGE

"If my speech tonight doesn't scare . . .": France, "Pictures from a Battlefield."
"One of the top AIDS doctors in the United States . . .": Hirshman, 195.
"I think I'm alive because of Larry Kramer and . . .": Bolerjack, interview with author,
   March 3, 2017.
"Together, gay men and lesbians forged . . .": Wyne.
"Mass Murder by Indifference" and "Center for Detention Camps.": Marty Robinson
   Collection.
"Test drugs, not people!" Faderman, 426.
"Being silent doesn't make the fear go away . . .": *Tongues Untied* (bonus footage).
"Turn fear into rage.": *Fight Back, Fight AIDS*.
Act up! Fight back! Fight AIDS!: Strub, 202.
"You don't speak *to* the media . . .": ibid.
"We are a diverse, non-partisan group . . .": ibid.
We advise and inform . . .: www.actupny.org.
"Everything ACT UP did it did analog . . .": Franke-Ruta.
we die and *they do nothing!*: *Fight Back, Fight AIDS*.
People with AIDS, under attack. What do we do?; *Act up! Fight back!*; *Healthcare is a right . . .*
   Healthcare is a right.; and *No more business as usual.*: ibid.
"If they stuck a microphone in your face . . .": Goldberg.
no violence, no violence.: *Fight Back, Fight AIDS*.
"jeans tight as a sunburn." France, *How to Survive a Plague* (book), 4.
"It was my life . . .": Hirshman, 200.
"I remember chanting . . .": Goldberg.

CHAPTER 9—COVERAGE

We'll never be silent again.: Goldberg.
"I love you.": Jones, *Stitching a Revolution*, 136.
"the greatest speech I've ever heard in my life.": *Fight Back, Fight AIDS*.
"During times when it was difficult . . .": McDarrah, 47.
"had an amazing capacity . . .": *Vito*.
"You could stay with his rant . . .": *After Stonewall*.

"it's time to pay attention . . .": Russo.

"If I'm dying from anything . . ."; "the 'real' people"; "the disposable populations . . ."; "don't spend their waking hours . . ."; and "They haven't been to two funerals . . .": ibid.

"Someday, the AIDS crisis will be over . . ." and "And then, after we kick . . .": ibid.

"We are being allowed to die . . .": ibid.

"shooting drugs"; "Some of the issues involved in this brochure . . ."; "I can easily understand that . . ."; and "I encourage you to practice . . .": "Understanding AIDS" (federal educational brochure).

"Anal intercourse, with or without a condom, is risky."; "You won't get AIDS from saliva, sweat, tears . . ."; "unprotected sex (without a condom) with an infected person."; and "Children hear about AIDS . . .": ibid.

CHAPTER 10—FURY

"I'm here today because I don't want a quilt . . .": *Fight Back, Fight AIDS*.

"If I die of AIDS—forget burial—. . .": http://www.treatmentactiongroup.org/history.

TIME *ISN'T* THE ONLY THING THE FDA IS KILLING and THE GOVERNMENT HAS BLOOD ON ITS HANDS. ONE AIDS DEATH EVERY HALF HOUR: *Fight Back, Fight AIDS*.

Seize control. Seize control.; *Forty-two thousand dead of AIDS, where was the FDA?*; *Release the drugs now. Release the drugs now.*; *We die / they do nothing. We die / they do nothing.*; and *Shame! Shame! Shame!*: ibid.

"unusual": "*Pneumocystis* pneumonia—Los Angeles."

"I'm horrified at the possibility . . .": Marty Robinson Collection (circa October 1989).

"dragging down the standards of all society.": Harden, 118.

KNOW YOUR SCUMBAGS and THIS ONE PREVENTS AIDS. Strub, 220–221.

CURB YOUR DOGMA and PAPAL BULL: ibid, 1.

CONDOMS NOT COFFIN: ibid, 1–2.

no violence, no violence: *Fight Back, Fight AIDS*.

"O'Connor, you're killing us . . .": Hirshman, 205.

"Safe sex is moral sex!"; "I support a woman's right to choose!"; and "Condoms save lives!": Strub, 3.

"May the Lord bless the man I love . . ." and "Opposing safe-sex education is murder.": ibid, 230.

CHAPTER 11—OUTLOOK

So if the quality fades . . .: *Fight Back, Fight AIDS*.

Let's go.; *This is war.*; *For the sick.*; *For the poor.*; *Act up!*; *Fight back!* and *Fight AIDS!*: ibid.

FAUCI, YOU'RE KILLING US.: Hirshman, 207.

"The country as a whole saw something . . .": *Fight Back, Fight AIDS*.

"For all the work that we've done . . .": ibid.

A CONDOM TO STOP UNSAFE POLITICS. HELMS IS DEADLIER THAN A VIRUS.: Strub, 256.

"never again proposed or passed . . .": ibid, 258.

"Plague! We are in the middle of . . .": *Fight Back, Fight AIDS*.

"We're *dying* . . .": France, *How to Survive a Plague* (book), 456.

"I feel your pain . . .": "The 1992 Campaign: Verbatim; Heckler Stirs Clinton Anger."

"I'll try to die a good death . . .": Howe.

"My name is Duane Kearns Puryear . . .": McDarrah, 147.

"turned people we love into ashes and bone chips . . .": *Fight Back, Fight AIDS.*

History will recall, Reagan and Bush did nothing at all.: ibid.

George Bush, you can't hide. We charge you with genocide.: ibid.

Bringing the dead to your door. We won't take it anymore.: ibid.

"When I saw him pressed . . .": ibid.

PART THREE—CONTROL

"As for Mark, when the living can no longer speak . . .": *How to Survive a Plague* (documentary).

CHAPTER 12—LOST

"I cannot in good conscience . . .": Specter, "How Magic Johnson Fought the AIDS Epidemic."

"What the hell are you afraid of? . . .": *Fight Back, Fight AIDS.*

"A miracle is possible, of course . . .": Schmalz, "Whatever Happened to AIDS?"

"Obviously you already know the 'big story' about me . . .": Riesenberg.

"Whenever I feel low . . .": *Absolutely Positive.*

CHAPTER 13—DRUGS

"This disease will be the end of many of us . . .": Kushner, *Angels in America* (Part Two), 148.

"It wasn't until we started putting the drugs in our bodies . . .": *How to Survive a Plague* (documentary).

"That breakthrough we thought was going to happen in '88 . . .": ibid.

"Death takes a holiday.": "Death takes a holiday" (editorial).

CHAPTER 14—REVIVAL

"Like any war . . .": *How to Survive a Plague* (documentary).

"survivor's bafflement.": Bolerjack, interview with author, March 25, 2017.

"I remember their names . . .": Cohen, "At Gathering of HIV/AIDS Pioneers. . . ."

"I miss so many people so bad.": *After Stonewall.*

"It jogs my memories . . .": Bolerjack, interview with author, March 3, 2017.

"An incomprehensible thing . . .": France, *How to Survive a Plague* (book), 512.

"To proclaim that anyone with HIV . . .": Bolerjack, *Pride, Politics & Plague*, 173.

CHAPTER 15—LEGACIES

"We hope to have such a vaccine ready . . .": Harden, 64.

"With other viruses, nature tells us . . .": ibid, 240–241.

"We have to make sure the next generation . . .": Cohen, "At Gathering of HIV/AIDS Pioneers. . . ."

"We're still in the midst of an epidemic.": ibid.

"You don't want to get this virus . . .": Strub, 431.

"You live or die by the pillbox.": Bolerjack, interview with author, March 25, 2017.

"I'm a young old man.": Leland, "'People Think It's Over.'"

"some genetic little glitch that went my way.": *Gay Sex in the 70s.*

"While many of us, through luck or circumstance . . .": France, *How to Survive a Plague* (book), 10.

"collective mass death experience": Franke-Ruta.

"For 20 years, I battled . . .": Sullivan.

"I had all this history with Bob Rafsky . . .": ibid.

"beaming like proud parents.": ibid.

"One of the things that brings the Recollectors together . . .": ibid.

"The quilt is the most democratic memorial ever made.": Rhoad.

"Every person who lived through those years . . .": Franke-Ruta.

"There was a time when we were all alive together.": ibid.

EPILOGUE

"Bury me furiously . . .": *Fight Back, Fight AIDS.*

"Let everyone here know . . .": *How to Survive a Plague* (documentary).

A NOTE FROM THE AUTHOR

"We're not surrounded by sadness . . .": Rhoad.

BIBLIOGRAPHY

BOOKS

Bolerjack, Steve. *Pride, Politics & Plague: Gay Life in Millennial New York City*, collection of columns published in the *New York Blade* 1998–2002. Lulu, 2011.

Faderman, Lillian. *The Gay Revolution: The Story of the Struggle*. New York: Simon & Schuster, 2015.

France, David. *How to Survive a Plague: The Inside Story of How Citizens and Science Tamed AIDS*. New York: Alfred A. Knopf, 2016.

Harden, Victoria A. *AIDS at 30: A History*. Washington, DC: Potomac Books, 2012.

Hirshman, Linda. *Victory: The Triumphant Gay Revolution*. New York: HarperCollins Publishers, 2012.

Johnson, Earvin "Magic," with William Novak. *My Life*. New York: Fawcett Books, Random House, Inc., 1992.

Jones, Cleve, with Jeff Dawson. *Stitching a Revolution: The Making of an Activist*. New York: HarperCollins and HarperSanFrancisco, 2000.

Jones, Cleve. *When We Rise: My Life in the Movement*. New York: Hachette Books, 2016.

McDarrah, Fred W., and Timothy S. McDarrah. *Gay Pride: Photographs from Stonewall to Today*. Chicago: A Cappella Books, 1994.

Quammen, David. *The Chimp and the River: How AIDS Emerged from an African Forest*. New York: W. W. Norton, 2015.

Shilts, Randy. *And the Band Played On: Politics, People, and the AIDS Epidemic*. New York: St. Martin's Press, 1987; twentieth anniversary edition, 2007.

Strub, Sean. *Body Counts: A Memoir of Activism, Sex, and Survival*. New York: Scribner, 2014.

DOCUMENTARIES, FILMS, AND PLAYS

Absolutely Positive. Documentary film written and directed by Peter Adair. Adair & Armstrong Productions, 1991.

After Stonewall. Documentary film directed by John Scagliotti. First Run Features, 1999.

The Age of AIDS. A Frontline documentary series produced and reported by Renata Simone. WGBH/Frontline, 2006.

Fight Back, Fight AIDS: 15 Years of ACT UP. Documentary by James Wentzy, 2002. Online supporting material at http://www.actupny.org/video/.

Gay Sex in the 70s. Documentary film produced and directed by Joseph Lovett. Wolfe Video LLC, 2006.

How to Survive a Plague. Documentary directed by David France. Public Square Films, 2012.

Kushner, Tony. *Angels in America: A Gay Fantasia on National Themes* ("Part One: Millennium Approaches"; "Part Two: Perestroika"). New York: Theatre Communications Group, Inc., 1992, 1993 (Part One) and 1992, 1994 (Part Two).

Living with AIDS. Documentary film produced and directed by Tina DiFeliciantonio. Naked Eye Productions, 1986.

Tongues Untied. Documentary film directed by Marlon Riggs. Signifyin' Works, 1989.

Vito. Produced and directed by Jeffrey Schwarz. Automat Pictures with HBO Documentary Films, 2011.

PRIMARY SOURCE DOCUMENTS

ACT UP New York. http://www.actupny.org.

Berkowitz, Richard, and Michael Callen (with editorial assistance by Richard Dworkin). *How to Have Sex in an Epidemic: One Approach*. New York: News from the Front Publications, May 1983.

Bolerjack, Steve. Author interview (telephone), March 3, 2017.

———. Author interview, Palm Springs, California, March 25, 2017.

Craig Rodwell Papers. Manuscripts and Archives Division, the New York Public Library. Astor, Lenox, and Tilden Foundations.

Goldberg, Ronald. Interview conducted by the Center for Artistic Activism, April 2016. https://artisticactivism.org/2016/04/ron-goldberg/.

Martin B. Duberman Papers. Manuscripts and Archives Division, the New York Public Library. Astor, Lenox, and Tilden Foundations.

Marty Robinson Collection. National History Archive, the Lesbian, Gay, Bisexual & Transgender Community Center, New York City.

Osmond, Dennis H. "Epidemiology of HIV/AIDS in the United States," HIV InSite Knowledge Base Chapter, March 2003. Data shared online at http://hivinsite.ucsf.edu/InSite?page=kb-01-03.

Rhoad, Julie. Author interview, Atlanta, Georgia, January 23, 2017.

Riesenberg, Michael. Personal correspondence with the author, 1993.

Ronald Reagan Presidential Library and Museum, Public Papers of the President.

Russo, Vito. "Why We Fight" speech, delivered May 9, 1988, Albany, New York.

Serko, David. *The David Serko Project: Activist Ron Goldberg Recalls the Act Up 1988 Wall Street II Action.* Online video at https://vimeo.com/41273190.

Steven J. Powsner Papers. National History Archive, the Lesbian, Gay, Bisexual & Transgender Community Center, New York City.

Summers, Todd, and Jennifer Kates. "Trends in U.S. Government Funding for HIV/AIDS—Fiscal Years 1981 to 2004." The Henry J. Kaiser Family Foundation, March 2004. Publication shared online at https://kaiserfamilyfoundation.files.wordpress.com/2013/01/issue-brief-trends-in-u-s-government-funding-for-hiv-aids-fiscal-years-1981-to-2004.pdf.

Treatment Action Group (TAG). http://www.treatmentactiongroup.org/history.

"Understanding AIDS." Educational brochure published by the U.S. Department of Health and Human Services, Centers for Disease Control, 1988.

MEDIA REPORTS AND NEWSPAPER, MAGAZINE, AND JOURNAL ARTICLES

"The 1992 Campaign: Verbatim; Heckler Stirs Clinton Anger: Excerpts From the Exchange." *New York Times*, March 28, 1992.

Ain, Morty. " 'I Didn't Think I'd See 30,' Says Greg Louganis." *ESPN The Magazine*, the Body Issue, 2016.

Altman, Lawrence K. "Rare Cancer Seen in 41 Homosexuals." *New York Times*, July 3, 1981.

Barnes, Edward, and Anne Hollister. "Now No One is Safe From AIDS." *LIFE*, July 1985.

Bernstein, Lenny. "The Graying of HIV: 1 in 6 New U.S. Cases Are People Older Than 50." *Washington Post*, April 16, 2016.

———. "'I Don't Feel Like I'm a Threat Anymore.' New HIV Guidelines Are Changing Lives." *Washington Post*, November 24, 2017.

Blair, Thomas R. "Safe Sex in the 1970s: Community Practitioners on the Eve of AIDS." *American Journal of Public Health*, June 2017.

Boynton, Andrew. "Remembering St. Vincent." *New Yorker*, May 16, 2013.

Buchanan, Patrick J. "AIDS Disease: It's Nature Striking Back." *New York Post*, May 24, 1983.

Callen, Michael, and Richard Berkowitz (with Richard Dworkin). "We Know Who We Are: Two Gay Men Declare War on Promiscuity." *New York Native*, November 8–21, 1982.

Cohen, Jon. "At Gathering of HIV/AIDS Pioneers, Raw Memories Mix with Current Conflicts." *Science*, October 2016.

———. "'We're in a mess.' Why Florida is struggling with an unusually severe HIV/AIDS problem." *Science*, June 13, 2018.

Crimp, Douglas. "Before Occupy: How AIDS Activists Seized Control of the FDA in 1988." *Atlantic*, December 6, 2011.

Dalton, Harlon L. "AIDS in Blackface." *Daedalus*, Vol. 118, No. 3 (Summer, 1989).

Daly, Michael. "AIDS Anxiety," *New York*, June 20, 1983.

Davis, David. "'Understanding AIDS'—The National AIDS Mailer." *Public Health Reports*, November–December 1991.

"Death takes a holiday" (editorial). *Bay Area Reporter* (San Francisco), August 13, 1998.

Doucleff, Michaeleen. "Researchers Clear 'Patient Zero' From AIDS Origin Story." National Public Radio: "Morning Edition," October 26, 2016.

Dunlap, David W. "As Disco Faces Razing, Gay Alumni Share Memories." *New York Times*, August 21, 1995.

———. "Michael Callen, Singer and Expert On Coping With AIDS, Dies at 38." *New York Times*, December 29, 1993.

Folkart, Burt A. "Dan Turner; Offered Hope to Those with AIDS." *Los Angeles Times*, June 6, 1990.

France, David. "Gay Samurai: Rodger McFarlane, Caretaker to the End." *New York*, May 24, 2009.

———. "Pictures from a Battlefield." *New York*, March 25, 2012.

Frankel, Joseph. "Trump Seems to Support Bush's AIDS Program for Now." *Atlantic*, February 8, 2017.

Franke-Ruta, Garance. "The Plague Years, in Film and Memory." *Atlantic*, February 24, 2013.

Hevesi, Dennis. "Rodger McFarlane, Who Led AIDS-Related Groups, Dies at 54." *New York Times*, May 18, 2009.

Holden, Stephen. "Vito Russo, 44; A Historian of Film and a Gay Advocate." *New York Times*, November 9, 1990.

Howe, Marvine. "Robert Rafsky, 47, Media Coordinator For AIDS Protesters." *New York Times*, February 23, 1993.

Johnson, Dirk. "Ryan White Dies of AIDS at 18; His Struggle Helped Pierce Myths." *New York Times*, April 9, 1990.

Kramer, Larry. "1,112 and Counting." *New York Native*, March 14–27, 1983.

———. "2,339 and counting" (advertisement). *Village Voice*, October 4, 1983.

Leland, John. "'People Think It's Over': Spared Death, Aging People With H.I.V. Struggle to Live." *New York Times*, June 1, 2013.

———. "Twilight of a Difficult Man: Larry Kramer and the Birth of AIDS Activism." *New York Times*, May 19, 2017.

McFarlane, Rodger. "Painful Truths: One veteran slut converts to sexual ecology." *POZ*, June 1997.

McKay, Tom. "In 1982, the White House Press Corps Thought AIDS Was a Joke," Mic .com, December 3, 2013. https://mic.com/articles/75363/in-1982-the-white-house -press-corps-thought-aids-was-a-joke#.JAZ65nt5z.

McNeil Jr., Donald G. "H.I.V. Arrived in the U.S. Long Before 'Patient Zero.'" *New York Times*, October 26, 2016.

"*Pneumocystis* pneumonia—Los Angeles." *Morbidity and Mortality Weekly Report* (*MMWR*), June 5, 1981.

Schmalz, Jeffrey. "The 1992 Elections: The States—the Gay Issues; Gay Areas Are Jubilant Over Clinton." *New York Times*, November 5, 1992.

———. "Whatever Happened to AIDS?" *New York Times* (Sunday magazine), November 28, 1993.

Sokol, Brett. "Club 57, Museum Piece: A bar that was once home to an East Village art movement time-travels to MoMA." *New York Times*, October 27, 2017.

Solomon, George. "Ex-Redskin Jerry Smith Says He's Battling AIDS; 'Maybe It Will Help People Understand.'" *Washington Post*, August 26, 1986.

Specter, Michael. "How Magic Johnson Fought the AIDS Epidemic." *New Yorker*, May 14, 2014.

———. "Postscript: C. Everett Koop, 1916–2013." *New Yorker*, February 26, 2013.

Sullivan, J. Courtney. "Adult Children of AIDS Victims Take Their Memories Out of the Shadows." *New York Times*, March 20, 2015.

Villarosa, Linda. "America's Hidden H.I.V. Epidemic." *New York Times Magazine*, June 11, 2017.

Wade, Nicholas. "Method and Madness; The Vindication of Robert Gallo." *New York Times*, December 26, 1993.

Weber, Bruce. "Spencer Cox, AIDS Activist, Dies at 44." *New York Times*, December 21, 2012.

Wickelgren, Ingrid. "Grad Student Produces AIDS Film." *Stanford Daily* (Stanford University), Palo Alto, California, November 15, 1985.

Wyne, Zaahira. "The Women Who Fought AIDS: 'It Was Never Not Our Battle.'" *Vice*, August 28, 2015.

A more complete bibliography may be found at the author's website, www.AnnBausum.com.

PHOTO CREDITS

Pages 2–3, 23: Courtesy Archives and Special Collections, University of California, San Francisco Library

Pages 7, 29, 39, 43, 98–99, 121, 129: Associated Press

Page 8: Kay Tobin, © Manuscripts and Archives Division, New York Public Library

Page 18: Courtesy Archives and Special Collections, University of California, San Francisco Library; photo by Jerry Telfer, *San Francisco Chronicle*

Pages 32–33: © John Schoenwalter

Pages 34–35, 63, 93, 109, 137: ACT UP New York, Manuscripts and Archives Division, New York Public Library

Page 43 (left): Ronald Reagan Library

Page 45: AIDS Education Posters, University of Rochester Library Special Collections, from the Alaska AIDS Prevention Project, Alaska Department of Health and Social Services and the Cooperative Extension Services, University of Alaska

Page 46: Courtesy Archives and Special Collections, University of California, San Francisco Library, and the San Francisco AIDS Foundation

Pages 48, 53: The Ted Sahl Archives: A Collection of San José Gay and Lesbian History, MSS-2001-01-01, courtesy San José State University Special Collections & Archives

Page 56: © Alon Reininger/Contact Press Images

Page 61: James Ruebsamen, Herald-Examiner Collection, Los Angeles Public Library

Page 69: Courtesy Ed Gamble, Ed Gamble Cartoon Collection, University of Tennessee Libraries, Knoxville

Page 73: Resource Center LGBT Archive, University of North Texas Libraries Special Collections

Page 76: © Rick Gerharter

Page 80: Courtesy Archives and Special Collections, University of California, San Francisco Library; AIDS Treatment News Records and John S. James, editor and publisher, AIDS Treatment News

Pages 85, 91, 101, 104: Associated Press, *Atlanta Journal-Constitution* Photographic Archive, Georgia State University Library

Page 88: Photo by Michael Abramson, LIFE Images Collection, Getty Images

Page 112: "Porchlight (Jay Funk & Mark Harrington)," all rights reserved © 2017 Stephen Barker

Page 124: Cold Spring Harbor Laboratory Archives

Page 134: Courtesy Sara Rafsky

Page 140: Gran Fury Collection, Manuscripts and Archives Division, New York Public Library

Page 147 (top and bottom): © Ann Bausum

INDEX

Poppers, 7, 24
POZ magazine, 54, 118
PrEP (pre-exposure
    prophylaxis), 130
Presidential elections
    1980, 19
    1984, 41
    1992, 95, 101–102
    1996, 102
Prison population, 130
Promiscuity, 18, 22, 24, 37, 40,
    46, 127
Prostitutes, 120
Protease, 110–112
Protease inhibitors, 111, 115,
    117
Protease paunch, 119
Puryear, Duane Kearns, 96

Quaaludes, 7

Racism, 82, 120
Rafsky, Bob, 93, 95–97, 99, 102,
    114, 134–135, 138–139
Rafsky, Sara, 102, 134–135
Ray family, 105–106
Reagan, Nancy, 42, 43
Reagan, Ronald, 19, 38, 41–43,
    46, 70, 76, 77, 114
Reagan administration, 19, 23,
    27, 38–39, 39, 42–43, 62,
    69–71
Recollectors, 134, 135
Red ribbons, 136, 137
Research, 23, 24, 28–30, 39,
    43, 44, 63–64, 70, 83, 91,
    93, 108–113, 123–125, 127,
    131, 132
Resnik, Debra, 74
Reverse transcriptase, 110–112,
    119
Rhoad, Julie, 51, 136
Riesenberg, Michael, 107
Riggs, Marlon, 107
Robinson, David, 96, 97, 102
Robinson, Marty, 62, 84, 105
Robinson, Max, 105
Rock, Nick, 12, 26
Roth, Marco, 135

Russo, Vito, 8, 35, 75–77, 79,
    88, 105

Safe sex, 21, 53, 86, 101
Saint disco, New York City, 7,
    15, 105
St. Patrick's Cathedral, New
    York City, 84, 86
St. Vincent's Hospital, New York
    City, 39, 55–56
San Francisco Bay Area Reporter,
    114
San Francisco Sentinel, 16
Sarandon, Susan, 83
Scharf, Kenny, 51
Schmalz, Jeffrey, 106
Scholastic, 83
Seize Control of the FDA
    protest, 79–80, 102
Senak, Mark, 21
Serodiscordant relationships, 131
Shanti Project, 21, 37
Shilts, Randy, 105, 127
Side effects of medications, 119
Sisters of Perpetual Indulgence,
    21, 23, 30, 31
Skin rash, 11, 16
Smallpox, 123
Smith, Jerry, 52
Smith, Willi, 105
Social Security, 109
Sonnabend, Joseph, 18, 31
Special K (ketamine), 7
Speed, 7
Staley, Peter, 79–80, 90, 94, 95,
    113, 117, 118, 133–135
Steptoe, John, 105
Stonewall riots (1969), 4–5, 8,
    19, 61, 140
Stop the Church action, 84–88
Storm the NIH action, 91–92,
    105
Strub, Sean, 38, 49, 54–58, 66,
    86, 94, 114, 118, 128
Studio 54, New York City, 7
Suicides, 57, 133, 136
Supreme Court of the United
    States, 60, 70, 89
Survivor's guilt, 117

Syphilis, 10

TAG (Treatment Action Group),
    95, 102, 133, 137
Tampons, 14
Taylor, Elizabeth, 83
T cells, 23, 110
Testing, 41, 46, 47–50, 62, 81,
    101, 113, 121, 122, 129–130
Tomlin, Lily, 75
Tongues Untied (film), 107
Toxic shock syndrome, 14
Toxoplasmosis, 12
Transgender movement, 5
Treatment + Data Committee
    (T+D), 89–91, 94–95
Truvada, 130
Tubman, Harriet, 107
Turner, Dan, 14, 30, 31, 50
Tuskegee study, 82

UNAIDS, 121, 122
"Understanding AIDS"
    (pamphlet), 77–78
University of California in San
    Francisco, 30

Village Voice, 36
Viral load tests, 113

Wallace, Joyce, 39
Washington Post, 52
Wave 3, 69
Waxman, Henry, 22
Weight loss, 12, 13, 37, 43
Wellikoff, Rick, 11, 12, 26
White, Ryan, 44, 46, 83, 105,
    106
White house lawn, ashes
    scattered on, 96–97,
    102–103
Wilson, Phil, 63
Wojnarowicz, David, 80,
    102–103
Wolfe, Maxine, 66
Women, HIV/AIDS and, 27, 39,
    50, 66, 83, 91, 100, 106, 130
Women's liberation movement, 5
World AIDS Day, 137